MW01488630

ANALYZING THE ISSUES

CRITICAL PERSPECTIVES ON
ABORTION

Edited by Anne C. Cunningham

Enslow Publishing

101 W. 23rd Street
Suite 240
New York, NY 10011
USA

Published in 2018 by Enslow Publishing, LLC
101 W. 23rd Street, Suite 240, New York, NY 10011

Library of Congress Cataloging-in-Publication Data
Names: Cunningham, Anne C., editor.
Title: Critical perspectives on abortion / edited by Anne C. Cunningham.
Description: New York : Enslow Publishing, [2018] | Series: Analyzing the
issues | Audience: Grade 9 to 12. | Includes bibliographical references
and index.
Identifiers: LCCN 2017001287 | ISBN 9780766084773 (library-bound)
Subjects: LCSH: Abortion--Juvenile literature. | Abortion--Moral and
ethical aspects. | Abortion.
Classification: LCC HQ767 .C742 2018 | DDC 362.1988/8--dc23
LC record available at https://lccn.loc.gov/2017001287

Printed in China

To Our Readers: We have done our best to make sure all website addresses
in this book were active and appropriate when we went to press. However,
the author and the publisher have no control over and assume no
liability for the material available on those websites or on any websites
they may link to. Any comments or suggestions can be sent by e-mail to
customerservice@enslow.com.

Excerpts and articles have been reproduced with the permission of the
copyright holders.

Photo Credits: Cover, Karen Bleier/AFP/Getty Images (abortion
demonstration), Thaiview/Shutterstock.com (background, pp. 4–5
background), gbreezy/Shutterstock.com (magnifying glass on spine);
p. 4 Ghornstern/Shutterstock.com (header design element, chapter start
background throughout book).

CONTENTS

INTRODUCTION

Forty-three years ago, the Supreme Court legalized abortion nationwide with its historic seven to two ruling in *Roe v. Wade*. Ever since, advocates of women's reproductive rights have sought to build on the *Roe* decision, expanding access to abortion services for all women regardless of age, race, or socioeconomic background. Opponents of abortion meanwhile have used every available legal, rhetorical, and emotional tool to obstruct any such easy access. This fierce struggle has made abortion one of the most divisive topics in American politics—the archetypal litmus test of one's progressive credentials or relative social, sexual, and religious conservatism. As this controversial topic shows no sign of having a neat resolution anytime soon, it is crucial to understand what both sides feel is at stake in the debate over abortion rights. From a variety of viewpoints, the articles compiled herein approach this question in ways we hope you will find illuminating.

Who exactly is fighting over abortion? According to a 2016 Pew Research poll, the American public is nearly split on the issue of abortion's legality. It is worth noting that less than a quarter of the population advocates extreme positions on either side, with 24 percent reporting abortion should always be legal, and only 16 percent favoring a total ban. Proponents of a woman's right to a legal abortion are generally referred to as "abortion rights advocates," or more commonly, "pro-choice." Those who oppose abortion self-identify as "pro-life," although pro-choice people prefer the term "abortion rights opponent," or "anti-choice," since "pro-life" is a vague term that often overlaps with other values (such as animal rights and pacifism, for example) held by those who nonetheless respect a woman's right to control her body and have autonomy over the reproductive process. Labels aside, these polls suggest that despite the divisiveness of the issue, common ground is indeed reachable, since the majority of Americans hold non-absolutist stances on abortion. As we will see however, Republican politicians and lawmakers have recently advanced extreme positions that are out of step with mainstream views, perhaps to energize the far right wing of their base. Although these attempts have largely been unsuccessful, they still prevent significant gains from being made on the advocacy front of women's reproductive health.

Prior to examining the pro and con sides of the abortion rights dispute, some historical context is warranted. There is evidence that abortion procedures have existed as early as ancient Egypt. In ancient Greece, the philosopher Aristotle suggested that an abortion early in a woman's pregnancy was a sensible plan for couples with more children than they could handle. In the contemporary era, American law descends from British common law, which held that abortion was legally acceptable as long it took place before the "quickening" period when fetal activity could be detected. This did not mean that abortion was always safe—far from it. Perhaps owing to many inept abortions that proved fatal to the mother, Connecticut became the first US state to outlaw the procedure in 1821. By 1965, abortion was illegal in every state, although a vast underground network of abortion providers continued to practice illicitly.

The social revolution ushered in by 1960s feminists and other social activism led to the legalization of abortion with *Roe*. The pushback was almost immediate. By 1976, Congress passed the Hyde Amendment prohibiting any federal funding, including Medicaid, from being used for abortions. Since an abortion costs upward of $400, and well over $1,000 after 20 weeks, this hurt poor women, often women of color, the most. Moreover, the Hyde Amendment restricted any funds from being earmarked for abortion research purposes, drastically altering the landscape of public health discourse and advocacy on the subject. Other countries such as Sweden have taken a radically different path. Could America ever follow such a progressive example?

Judging by recent events, the answer to the above question is a resounding "not likely." In 2015, Congress passed the Pain Capable Unborn Child Protection Act, otherwise known as HR 36. This law restricted any abortion after 20 weeks of pregnancy, unless the life of the mother is in danger, or in cases of rape or incest. While there is some evidence that a fetus has brain activity before 25 weeks, we do not know conclusively that a fetus at this stage of development can feel and understand pain, as it lacks a developed central nervous system. The emotional appeal to fetal pain is typical of abortion opponents, as is a superficial concern with the health and safety of the mother. This is the stated motivation behind Texas law HB 2, which was struck down as unconstitutional, and which stipulated minimum size requirements for abortion clinics that would make it almost impossible for most clinics to stay open. Similar laws have also been passed in Ohio and about twelve additional states. That these laws were overturned indicates that abortion rights advocates are vindicated in their belief that the best way to care for the health and safety of a pregnant woman is to provide her with the most accurate information possible. Should she choose abortion within the allotted time frame, it is difficult to argue that a safe and affordable abortion serves anything other than these interests.

Despite these developments, we can expect abortion opponents to continue their efforts to chip away at legality. Although ulterior motives for doing so remain speculative, the best way for advocates of women's health to counter these measures is to have the best information and arguments at their disposal. For the many who oppose abortion on religious or other grounds, we respect these views, but encourage the development of tolerance for the plurality of views that exist on the subject, and the resistance of any arguments based on morality.

CHAPTER 1

WHAT ACADEMICS, EXPERTS, AND RESEARCHERS SAY

Abortion rights remain a battleground issue within contemporary social and scientific research. Though a woman's right to have an abortion within 24 weeks of conception has been constitutionally protected since 1973, abortion opponents have not accepted this lying down. At state and local levels, abortion opponents have deployed numerous tactics to restrict practical and safe access to abortion services. Perhaps the most successful of such restrictions was the Hyde Amendment. Passed in 1976, this law banned Medicaid from covering abortions. In addition, the Hyde Amendment also prohibits any federal funding to go toward abortion-related research.

Though a woman's decision to have an abortion is a private matter, the aggregate of each individual decision has relevant public health implications. As such, we might expect the US government to reverse course and take an active role in collecting and disseminating accurate information on the issue. Unfortunately, this is not the case. Due to the aforementioned restrictions on the use of federal funds for abortion-related science, all such research in the US is privately funded. Thus, an already heavily contested field of research, at times responsible for steering public and legal discourse on abortion policy, is subject to much polarizing bias and misinformation.

Regardless of underlying motives, the pro-life position hinges on the belief that person-hood begins at conception, and therefore abortion is tantamount to murder. Since the question of when life begins is riddled with philosophical speculation and religious dogma, it is difficult to settle conclusively. Thus, the pro-life side requires copious research and anecdotal evidence to back up their position. Some have raised doubts as to the veracity and methodology of their information.

Pro-choice groups typically cite research telling a much different story. Indeed, multiple peer-reviewed studies have proven that women seeking an abortion in the first trimester face few health risks—unless, of course, they do not have access to safe, legal, and professional clinics.

The opening argument in this chapter comes from Joerg Dreweke of The Guttmacher Institute, a leading pro-choice organization. Dreweke argues that widespread and effective contraceptive use caused a decline in unintended pregnancies. This counters the claim that the culture is moving in a "pro-life" direction, and that restrictions on abortions have been effective in preventing them. Next, former director of University of California at San Francisco's Advancing New Standards in Reproductive Health (ANSIRH) Tracy Weitz discusses some recent findings, as well as new tactics opponents are using to make abortion less available and convenient for women. Finally, we will hear from Northern Arizona University professor Sanjam Ahluwalia, who places the US abortion discourse of choice and sexual modernity in a global, postcolonial perspective.

"NEW CLARITY FOR THE U.S. ABORTION DEBATE: A STEEP DROP IN UNINTENDED PREGNANCY IS DRIVING RECENT ABORTION DECLINES," BY JOERG DREWEKE, FROM *GUTTMACHER POLICY REVIEW*, MARCH 18, 2016

[EDITOR'S NOTE: NO CHARTS ARE INCLUDED IN THIS VERSION OF THE TEXT. HOWEVER, CHARTS CAN BE ACCESSED AT THE ORIGINAL ARTICLE ON THE GUTTERMACHER POLICY REVIEW WEBSITE.]

HIGHLIGHTS

- The abortion decline between 2008 and 2011 was driven by a steep drop in unintended pregnancy, which in turn is most plausibly explained by more and better contraceptive use.
- New evidence contradicts arguments by abortion opponents that the 2008-2011 abortion decline resulted from more women carrying unintended pregnancies to term because of state abortion restrictions or because they chose to do so of their own accord.
- These findings have major implications for the U.S. abortion debate as, among other things, they validate that supporting and expanding women's access to contraceptive services leads to a lower incidence of abortion.

Using any contraceptive method significantly reduces a woman's likelihood of becoming pregnant, and the most effective methods virtually eliminate that risk. This common-sense notion is supported by the scientific evidence,

11

as well as by the life experience of tens of millions of American women and couples who have used contraceptives to time and space their childbearing or avoid pregnancy altogether. And yet, a perennial argument put forth by abortion opponents at the federal and state levels holds that contraception does not reduce unintended pregnancy—nor the incidence of abortion—and may actually increase it by leading to more sexual activity and, therefore, more risk.

This argument surfaces regularly in various contexts, including the debate over defunding Planned Parenthood, a leading U.S. provider of contraceptive care and other vital services. During a September 2015 hearing in the U.S. House of Representatives, Rep. James Sensenbrenner (R-WI) said "Well, I don't think there's statistics that indicated that that's the case" in response to a witness who argued that "it makes no sense not to fund [contraceptive] services if you want to reduce the number of abortions."[1]

Much the same happened in February 2014, when the Guttmacher Institute released a study finding that the U.S. abortion rate had dropped 13% between 2008 and 2011.[2] Given that birthrates had also declined substantially during that time, the authors hypothesized that fewer women were experiencing unintended pregnancies. In addition, the evidence suggested that more women were using highly effective contraceptive methods, which further supported the idea that fewer women were having unintended pregnancies thanks to better contraceptive use. At the time, too, abortion-rights opponents disputed that the trend could have been driven by declines in unintended pregnancy generally and by improvements in contraceptive use in particular.

ARGUMENTS DEBUNKED

In explaining the 2008-2011 abortion decline, antiabortion activists pointed to the spike in abortion restrictions that started in 2011.[3-5] Indeed, between 2011 and 2013, states enacted 205 abortion restrictions; however, this surge in restrictions obviously could not have played a significant role in reducing abortion incidence retroactively. The abortion declines which occurred in 2008-2011 predated the bulk of these new restrictions, with most of them not taking effect until late 2011 or after. Also, abortion rates declined in 44 states and the District of Columbia, including many with few if any restrictions, such as California and New York.

New data further bolster the case that restrictions were not a main factor in the abortion decline. The mechanism by which restrictions would lead to fewer abortions is to force or otherwise compel women to carry an unwanted pregnancy to term. If that were the case, one would expect to see fewer women who experience an unintended pregnancy having abortions. One would also expect an increase in births, and in unplanned births in particular. Neither of these happened during 2008-2011.

Rather, according to Guttmacher Institute research published in the *New England Journal of Medicine* (*NEJM*) in 2016, the proportion of unintended pregnancies ending in abortion did not decline between 2008 and 2011, but stayed relatively stable at 40-42%. Likewise, the rate of unplanned births dropped by almost one-fifth, from 27 to 22 unplanned births per 1,000 women of reproductive age (15-44).[6] Unplanned birth rates declined notably among the groups of women who experience the highest rates of abortion: blacks and Hispanics, and those who are low income, cohabiting, have low educational attainment or are in their 20s.

With unplanned birth rates down across virtually all demographic groups and the proportion of unintended pregnancies ending in abortion stable across virtually all groups, unplanned births were clearly not replacing abortions to any significant extent during this period. This, in turn, strongly suggests that the 2008-2011 abortion decline was not due to abortion restrictions.

Abortion opponents have also asserted that, beyond restrictions, the 2008-2011 abortion decline was the result of a growing "culture of life," that is, a broad shift in public sentiment against abortion that has prompted more women—in particular, young women of a supposed "prolife generation"—to carry an unintended pregnancy to term.[7] The most recent evidence, however, clearly contradicts this claim. Among teenagers aged 15-19, the percentage of unintended pregnancies ending in abortion remained virtually unchanged between 2008 and 2011 (37-38%).[6] It also stayed unchanged (at 42%) for those aged 25-29, and even increased slightly (from 41% to 44%) for women aged 20-24 (see chart). In short, among young women as well as women overall, the proportion of unintended pregnancies ending in abortion did not decrease between 2008 and 2011, and the unplanned birth rate fell rather than rose. Taken together, these data provide strong evidence against the claim that the 2008-2011 abortion decline was driven by antiabortion sentiment.

Antiabortion activists did not wait for these data on unintended pregnancy to be available and instead tried to explain the 2008-2011 abortion decline using a different—

and insufficient—statistic that was available earlier: the proportion of all pregnancies (rather than unintended pregnancies) ending in abortion. This proportion fell from 23 abortions per 100 pregnancies in 2008 to 21 per 100 in 2011.[2] Abortion opponents often erroneously argue that the only possible reason for a decline in this ratio (sometimes called the "abortion ratio") is that more women decide or are made to carry an unintended pregnancy to term, but the new evidence shows that this was not the case.[6] Rather, this ratio declined because a smaller proportion of all pregnancies were unintended, which in turn resulted in fewer pregnancies ending in abortion.

BEHIND THE ABORTION DECLINE

Indeed, the *NEJM* study found that the U.S. unintended pregnancy rate declined 18% between 2008 and 2011— reaching its lowest level in at least three decades. The proportion of U.S. pregnancies that were unintended fell to 45%, down from 51% in 2008. As a result of fewer unintended pregnancies, the rates of both abortion and unplanned birth fell substantially over the period, by 13% and 18%, respectively (see chart). This new evidence goes a long way toward settling the debate over why U.S. abortion incidence declined between 2008 and 2011.

The *NEJM* study was designed to monitor trends in unintended pregnancy over time, not to pinpoint the reasons behind any changes, but the authors speculate about several factors that might have contributed to the decline they observed.

Changes in sexual behavior? The authors do not consider changes in sexual behavior to have played any significant role, noting that the frequency of sexual activity does not tend to change much among adults. Comprehensive data on adult sexual activity for the 2008-2011 period are not yet available. But among women aged 15-44, various indicators of sexual behavior—such as ever having had sex with a male partner and the number of male sexual partners within the last 12 months—were similar in 2006-2008 compared with 2002.[8] Also, levels of teen sexual activity did not change during 2008-2011.[9]

Demographic shift? Another possible explanation is a shift in the population toward groups that are at lower risk of unintended pregnancy. However, the opposite happened during 2008-2011:The proportion of U.S. women in groups with historically higher rates of unintended pregnancy, such as poor and Hispanic women, increased.[10,11] In other words, the overall decline in unintended pregnancy rates happened despite—not because of—these population changes, which makes such significant declines over a short period even more notable.

Greater desire for pregnancy? As a third possible explanation, the authors noted a slightly greater desire for pregnancy, possibly a consequence of the U.S. economy improving after the 2007-2009 recession. However, the authors believe this increase in the intended pregnancy rate only made a small contribution to the unintended pregnancy decline, given that this increase was small compared with the decline in the unintended pregnancy rate.

Better contraceptive use. There is considerable evidence, on the other hand, that changes in contraceptive use are a plausible explanation for the decline in unintended pregnancy and subsequent abortion.

First, overall use of any contraceptive method increased slightly among women at risk of unintended pregnancy, from 89% in 2008 to 90% in 2012.[12,13] Even such a seemingly small increase in contraceptive use can have a measurable impact on unintended pregnancy and abortion rates. Research shows that among all women at risk of unintended pregnancy, the 14% who do not practice contraception over the course of a given year or have long gaps in use account for more than half (54%) of all unintended pregnancies (see chart).[14]

Second, and perhaps more important, women's use of highly effective contraceptive methods—such as the IUD and implant—has shot up in recent years,[15] including during the 2008-2011 period when unintended pregnancy and abortion fell sharply. These highly effective contraceptive methods are often referred to as LARCs, or long-acting reversible contraceptives.

Use of these methods, especially the IUD, more than tripled between 2007 and 2012, from 3.7% of all contraceptive users to 11.6% (see chart, page 20).

Women weigh many factors when choosing a method, but LARC methods have several important strengths: They are more than 99% effective at preventing pregnancy, may last up to 12 years and do not require women to remember to use their method every day or every time they have sex. Increased use of methods that virtually guarantee consistent and error-free use is a critical development, given that the 18% of women who use contraception inconsistently—for example, by forgetting to take the pill every day or not using a condom every time they have sex—account for 41% of all unintended pregnancies.[14] Increases in LARC use likely led to more consistent and effective contraceptive use overall, contributing to the decline in the unintended pregnancy rate.

In short, the evidence is considerable that more and better contraceptive use is the key driver of the 2008-2011 declines in unintended pregnancy and abortion. These trends among all U.S. women appear to echo earlier trends that have helped drive pregnancy, birth and abortion rates among U.S. teens to record lows. Research shows that the teen pregnancy declines between 1995 and 2002 were overwhelmingly the result of improvements in contraceptive use, with contraception accounting for 86% of the decline (and teens delaying sex for the remaining 14%).[16] Even more so, the continued teen pregnancy declines between 2003 and 2010—a period with no changes in teen sexual activity—were entirely due to contraceptive use.

BEYOND 2011

Without current, comprehensive data on trends in contraceptive use, unintended pregnancy and abortion, it is impossible to know with any certainty what has happened in the period since 2011. Available abortion incidence data are incomplete, but they do suggest that the U.S. abortion rate has continued its long-term decline beyond 2011. A report from the *Associated Press*, which contacted state health departments to get their latest available abortion data, shows abortion declines across a broad swath of states through at least 2013.[17] Similarly, data from the Centers for Disease Control and Prevention show a continued national decline through 2012.[18]

Several factors are likely contributing to this continued abortion decline. The evidence is strong that state abortion restrictions played no significant role in the 2008-2011 abortion decline, as discussed earlier; however, state restrictions may have had an impact in the post-2011 period. Most restrictions do not keep large numbers of women from obtaining an abortion, but the most burdensome restrictions—such as bans on Medicaid coverage of abortion or requiring women to make two separate trips to an abortion provider—can measurably reduce incidence.[19,20] Abortion opponents have embarked on a concerted effort to raise the economic cost of obtaining an abortion, including by layering various types of restrictions on top of each other and through regional clustering of restrictions to make it difficult for women to obtain care in a neighboring state.[21,22] This use of coercive laws to make women carry an unwanted pregnancy to term is likely to have had a measurable impact on abortion incidence in some states in the post-2011 period. For instance, one study suggests that a 2013 Texas law that shuttered almost half the state's facilities that provide abortion care may have contributed to a decline in abortion incidence.[23]

Still, there is good reason to believe that abortion has continued to decline since 2011, and that continued declines in unintended pregnancy are a factor. For instance, based on the limited available data that the *Associated Press* gathered, it is notable that abortion appears to have continued to decline even in states that have few or no abortion restrictions, such as New York, Oregon and Washington.[17,21] This could be an indication of further, broad-based declines in unintended pregnancy, but it will need to be confirmed using more comprehensive and accurate data.

Another reason to be optimistic about the likelihood of fewer unintended pregnancies since 2011 is the potential for improvements in contraceptive use accompanying the advent of the Affordable Care Act (ACA). Thanks to the ACA, the proportion of U.S. women of reproductive age who are uninsured dropped by more than one-fifth between 2013 and 2014, driven primarily by gains in Medicaid coverage.[24] The ACA has also spurred significant improvements in private insurance plans' contraceptive coverage, leading to a steep decline in out-of-pocket costs for hormonal IUDs,[25] the pill and other popular methods,[26] and saving U.S. women nearly half a billion dollars in out-of-pocket costs for contraception in 2013 alone.[27] Collectively, this evidence illustrates that more women can now choose a birth control method on the basis of which works best for them—as opposed to which they can afford.

It will likely take years until sufficient data are available to know what has happened since 2011 and why. The factors driving changes in abortion incidence will also differ significantly among states. For instance, some states—such as Maine, Ohio, Oklahoma and Texas—have made it more difficult for women to avoid unintended pregnancy in the first place, either by directly cutting funding for family planning services for low-income residents or by making it more difficult for specialized family planning providers to access public funds.[28] Attempts to defund Planned Parenthood may be having a serious impact as well. In 2011, Texas banned health centers from participating in its women's health program if they provide abortion or are associated with a provider that does.

As a consequence, the program served far fewer women in 2013 than in 2011.[29] Similar attempts to defund Planned Parenthood have flared at both the federal and state levels. Although it is unclear to what extent these attacks can or will succeed, the potential impact on access to contraceptive services could be severe.[30]

However, even as the post-2011 picture remains murky, evidence from the 2008-2011 period validates the common-sense notion that supporting and expanding women's access to family planning services not only protects U.S. women's health and rights, it also reduces abortion rates.

1. What factors led to a reduction in abortion rates between 2008 and 2011, according to the author?

2. How does evidence in this article contradict some of the claims of abortion-rights opponents?

"AMID ABORTION DEBATE, THE PURSUIT OF SCIENCE," BY NINA MARTIN, FROM *PROPUBLICA*, JANUARY 7, 2014

For the last decade or so, Tracy Weitz has been one of the most prominent abortion researchers in the United States.

As director of the University of California at San Francisco's Advancing New Standards in Reproductive

Health (ANSIRH), part of the Bixby Center for Global Reproductive Health, she has co-authored seven studies in major journals in the past year alone, on topics ranging from how low-income women pay for abortions to why some women who want an abortion delay until it is too late.

This summer, one of the studies she oversaw persuaded California lawmakers to allow trained non-doctors (nurse practitioners, certified midwives, physician assistants) to perform first-trimester abortions, possibly the biggest expansion of abortion access since the Food and Drug Administration approved the abortion pill in 2000.

Now, just as some of ANSIRH's most ground-breaking work is starting to see the light of day, Weitz is leaving the world of clinical research. She has taken a job at an organization she declined to name but where she hopes her impact on women's reproductive health issues will be broader and deeper.

Weitz recently spoke with ProPublica's Nina Martin. This conversation has been edited and amended for clarity and brevity.

NM: How did abortion become the main focus of your work? What is your background?

TW: I'm a medical sociologist by training. I started off trying to figure out how to deliver health care services. I did that for many years as an administrator and was frustrated that we seemed to just be rearranging the deck chairs on the Titanic. I also have a real interest in policy and politics. Abortion for me has always been the natural place in which all of those things come together. It is a political issue. It is a social issue. It is a health care issue. It is a feminist issue.

NM: What are some of the main challenges to doing abortion research in this country?

TW: The federal government has a prohibition on funding any research that involves abortion care. You cannot get funding from the National Institutes of Health to study, say, abortion techniques — how to make it safer. But this ban has been interpreted very, very broadly to preclude funding *anything* involving abortion, even a topic like women's emotional responses. That has left the funding of research on abortion to the philanthropic community.

Now, it's very unusual for foundations to fund clinical research. It's not historically what they do — research is the domain of government. But in the last 10 years, there's been recognition in the philanthropic community that in order to make progress [on reproductive rights], whether culturally or politically or in the service-delivery arena, there are research questions that we need to answer.

This [private funding] has opened up an enormous avenue for researchers who are interested in questions about abortion care, abortion policy, and abortion in American culture. But it comes with its own downside, which is that people are very suspect of research that is funded by organizations that have particular ideological agendas.

NM: As researchers, what kind of hurdles and antagonism do you face?

TW: There's definitely a difference between the social scientists who do the research and the MDs who actually do abortions. Abortion doctors have had assassinations, barricades and constant protesters. As researchers, our safety hasn't really been in question.

Most of the harassment comes at the level of trying to discount our academic reputation— suggesting that anyone who does abortion-related research who believes that abortion should be legal shouldn't be trusted. That somehow our science is tainted, that we haven't used good methods. That's why we have a strong interest in being published in the peer-reviewed literature. We think that the science should be open to scrutiny. It should be put through the same kind of rigor that other clinical or social research is.

NM: Let's talk about the study that has probably had the greatest impact so far: the one looking at whether trained non-doctors—nurses, midwives, physicians assistants —can safely perform vacuum-aspiration abortions in the first trimester. That study included nearly 20,000 patients throughout California—one of the largest studies on abortion ever done in the United States. The study had two key findings. First, it found almost no difference in complication rates in abortions done by doctors versus non-doctors. Second, the overall rate of complications for both groups was very low—much lower than abortion opponents claim. Has the study shed light on other abortion-related issues as well?

TW: Yes. One has to do with hospital transfers [patients who require hospital care after having an abortion]. We were interested in this topic, of course, because it's a category of complication, and you want to track it. But it wasn't something we intended to focus on.

Then states [including Texas] started passing new laws that require physicians who offer abortion care to have admitting privileges to hospitals. And we realized that, thanks to [the non-doctor] study, we had very good data showing that complications requiring transfers to hospitals are actually exceedingly rare.

Of about 20,000 patients over several years, only four were directly transferred.

NW: There's a second study I want to talk about, which is known as the Turnaway Study. It's a long-term study looking at what happens when women who want an abortion can't get one. They show up at a clinic too late and are turned away.

TW: First some background. At the Bixby Center and ANSIRH, we are driven by three sets of issues and concerns. One is: How can care be best delivered? That's the question underlying the non-physician study. We're very interested in safety in general. Do you need to be in an ambulatory surgery center? Do you need to have a nurse who administers anesthesia? Which kinds of cervical preparations are safe and do the least damage to the cervix?

Two, we care a lot about women's experiences. We know that 1 in 3 women are going to have an abortion in their lifetime. And choosing to be a parent or not is a big decision. Whatever a woman decides, we want to know what can improve their outcomes. What do they need from their social networks and their friends? What are the long-term effects of silence and secrecy?

The third area of interest is social inequities. Where is there uneven distribution of services, uneven distribution of economic outcomes?

The Turnaway Study arose out of the second and third set of concerns. Abortion opponents have been pushing the idea that abortion hurts women, that they feel regret. With 1.3 million women having an abortion every year, it's likely that a certain number do feel regret. That's the natural curve of any kind of big decision. What we want to know is: Who are those women and what do they need?

But another of our questions was: what happens to women who wanted an abortion but couldn't get one? What happens to her economically, what happens to her psychologically, what happens to her other kids? That was the underlying question behind the Turnaway Study.

NM: Can you summarize the findings so far?

TW: The take-home from that study is that most women are having an abortion because they say they can't afford to have a child. And it turns out that they're right: Two years later, women who had a baby they weren't expecting to have, compared to the women who had the abortion they wanted, are three times more likely to be living in poverty. They knew they couldn't afford a kid and it turns out they were correct.

NM: Can you give some specifics about how the study was designed?

TW: The principal investigator is Diana Greene Foster, who was trained as a demographer. It is an eight-year study and includes about 30 abortion facilities in every region of the country. The sole criteria was that the clinic had to be isolated—it had to be the only one within 150 miles that was willing to do abortions up to whatever it set as its gestational limit [the latest point at which it will terminate a pregnancy]. So if a woman was turned away from that facility, she really had no other option. She probably was going to have that baby.

We recruited about 1,000 women—that alone took us three years. About a quarter were women who had been turned away and had a baby they weren't expecting. Approximately 500 were women who happened to be just under the gestational limit when they arrived at the clinic so were able to get the abortion they wanted. They were the comparison group.

We also wanted to know if women receiving earlier abortions were somehow different. So the remaining participants—about 250—are women who received first-trimester abortions.

We followed the women every six months for five years — a phone interview with a very lengthy survey that includes every question we could think of about their mental health, their economic circumstances, using routine and standardized tools, so we have some basis for comparison. Everyone in the study has finished at least two years, and some women have completed their five years and are rolling off.

NM: What has been your most eye-opening finding?

TW: The study has really exposed how hard it is to be a parent in this country. It is a huge economic investment. And if you don't have the economic resources to be a parent, there's nothing to help you.

Data from the study is also helping to answer other questions for which we have no good research until now—for example, how women feel about mandatory ultrasounds before an abortion and what factors contribute to some women feeling regret afterwards.

NM: Finally, I want to talk about some preliminary research you presented at a conference last fall, looking at how state and federal courts view the kind of research you are working on.

TW: ANSIRH was started specifically to ensure that health policy is grounded in evidence. Because many laws aimed at restricting abortion were ending up in the courts, I became interested in how judges were interpreting the science in their legal decisions. We focused on four abortion-related issues where the science is pretty clear—whether women are at risk for suicide after abortion, gestational bans based on the presumption that the fetus feels pain, ultrasound-viewing mandates, and medical abortion regimens.

We looked through over a thousand documents—including lawsuits, briefs, rulings by courts at every level, the scientific studies that are referenced, the CVs of the medical experts whose work was cited. We analyzed not just the court decisions, but their language about the scientific claims, how expert knowledge is referenced, the quality of the research, whether the studies appeared in peer-reviewed journals—that kind of thing. We've really just scratched the surface—we had no idea how much there would be out there.

NM: What have you found?

TW: There is no consistent standard for how science is or is not incorporated into the legal decisions. Across the decisions, the same scientific studies are adjudicated very differently. Overwhelmingly what we do see is political ideology substituted for objective standards in adjudicating scientific claims. We were very disheartened to find that many of the judicial decisions were discounting the science altogether. I think I was a little naive. I had this idea that the courts were more objective.

Since I started this work, I've been intrigued to discover that there's a whole body of criticism—a lot of it around climate change—over whether courts should have anything to do with science. When the D.C. federal court was set up, all the patent cases went there. There was a recognition that these issues were really complicated— more science-y—and you needed to have judges who had specific expertise to decide them. Now, whether they're about environmental science or, in our case, health-related science, these cases are being spread out across multiple courts, and judges with absolutely no scientific training are being asked to make adjudications about science. Should we be training judges to review science? Should we be thinking about specialty courts with scientific expertise?

One of the more troubling findings is the way that controversy has become a reason to discount science. There's a great book called "Merchants of Doubt" [Naomi Oreskes and Erik Conway, Bloomsbury, 2011]. It's about the production of scientific controversy as a way to discount legitimate scientific research and clear-cut consensus about tobacco or climate change, but it also applies to abortion. As the book points out, you don't need to disprove science anymore. All you need to do is suggest that the science is actually in doubt. Courts will then look at and say, "It's a controversy, so deference should go to the Legislature," or "It's a controversy, so we'll do whatever we want."

A contributing problem is that, in the legal context, medical experts and scientists who do abortion or study abortion have been seen as suspect. Lisa Harris, at the University of Michigan, has written some great stuff on what she calls "The Legitimacy Paradox." It goes like this: By virtue of doing an abortion, you're not a real doctor. Therefore, real doctors don't do abortions. Therefore, you have the right to regulate them because they're not real doctors.

NM: That brings me to the last thing I want to talk about, which is the issue of stigmatization. That's a major thread in your research and writings. Why is this issue is so important to you?

TW: A stigma is a mark that makes you seen as morally suspect. It's not just bad. It's bigger than bad.

In the abortion context, stigmatization means that your position on abortion says everything about you as a human being. To do abortion means that you are morally corrupt. The fact that you would have an abortion means you're a different kind of person. And the consequences associated with disclosure—whether it's "I support legal abortion," "I do abortions," "I've had an abortion"—now carry huge social weight. That leads to silence.

Now, I'm a person who fundamentally believes in doing anything that I can to help women have their families when they want to have their families. If I can help her figure out how she gets the contraception she wants and she picks the partners she wants and she has the money she wants so that she never has to have an abortion, then I've been a success.

But if she needs an abortion, she needs an abortion. And I'm there for her with that support. I've never met a woman who said, "It's on my bucket list to have an abortion."

I want everyone to have every tool in their tool-box to be able to have a family, when and if they want to. Any of those strategies are legitimate strategies. That includes abortion.

1. Why is funding for abortion research in the US so limited, problematic, and even suspect?

2. If courts are reluctant to take conclusive scientific research as fact, what problems might this cause for cases involving women's reproductive rights and health?

"ABORTION AND GAY MARRIAGE: SEXUAL MODERNITY AND ITS DISSONANCE IN THE CONTEMPORARY WORLD," BY SANJAM AHLUWALIA, FROM *ECONOMIC & POLITICAL WEEKLY*, DECEMBER 21, 2015

I would like to thank my Women and Gender Studies students, Kamalam Unninayar and Smita Bhatnagar, for the luxury to rehearse many of these arguments. Thanks to Antoinette Burton for positive comments on a draft. Sanjay Joshi made time to provide invaluable feedback. I thank him for his intellectual generosity and sustained intimacy over the years.

The contemporary moment of sexual politics is marked by intense volatility and internal fissures, evident in the furious media reporting and multiple commentaries on social networks. Gay marriage and abortion are particular instantiations within the sexual landscape that have caught my attention, for their distinctly different political and discursive trajectories. These two issues highlight the underlying incoherence and fault lines within the contemporary sexual landscape, locally and globally.

The politics of sexual modernity today seems riddled with glaring contradictions, hard to reconcile within a transformative feminist framework. Gay marriage and gay-friendliness is fast becoming a distinct marker of modernity, progress, and Western liberalism.[1] Western nations appear to be virtually tripping over each other in seeking to claim their global leadership vis-a-vis their gay-friendly state policies. Ireland is the most recent member of the Western world to claim its place as the first nation to legalise gay marriage through a referendum (Hakim and Dalby 2015). Nations are deploying gay politics to self-represent themselves as agents of progressive sexual politics and to mark their distinctions from the sexually illiberal "other."

For instance, Israel has effectively deployed a self-serving gay-friendly platform to mark itself off from Palestinians and its Arab citizens. Gay politics has been co-opted into the service of the Israeli state, allowing it to pink-wash its sustained apartheid policies (Puar 2011 and Schulman 2012). Britain has threatened to withdraw financial aid from some African countries, based on what it reads as their purported homophobia (Rao 2014;BBC

News 2011). Iran, of course, has been demonised as an anti-gay Muslim country, similar to the stereotyping of Palestinians (Najmabadi 2012). Russia in the post-Cold War period is othered on the basis of its unfriendliness towards gay people (Sochi 2014; Baer 2002). On a more local level within the United States, minority communities are similarly represented as being homophobic (Dhawan 2013). All of these representations are, of course, in contrast to the always-already progressive, modern and liberal mindedness of the hegemon-Western nations and the primarily Caucasian publics their leaderships address.

Contemporary championing of gay politics presents a jarring reversal of historical narratives on sexual scripts of the 19th and early 20th centuries. In the not so recent past, certain groups and cultures were deemed culturally inferior and as such marked as sexual "others," for their practices of intimacy and desires that were in contrast to those of dominant homophobic Western sexual codes.

For instance, Muslims of the 19th and early 20th centuries were marked as sodomites and as such seen as backward and barbaric, compared to the then intensely homophobic West (Massad 2002). Russia, in its past as the demonic Union of Soviet Socialist Republics, was accused of fostering internal dissent within the capitalist Western world through its encouragement of homosexuality (Shibusawa 2012). In the contemporary moment Russia continues to be the "other" of the Western world, but this time, the sexual discourse is flipped to mark Russia as a culture embracing and advocating anti-gay homophobic policies and sentiments. As such, Russia once again finds itself in a misstep with the acceptable Western sexual norm.

Colonised Africa operated as a sexual other of the "civilised" Western world due to its putative hypersexuality, but today African countries such as Uganda and Malawi (Long 2011) are othered for their sexual conservatism and homophobia. India, as the orientalised sexual fantasy of the 19th and 20th century, is also seen as not being in step with the changing sexual tide. Anti-sodomy laws continue to be on the books in postcolonial India, ironically, themselves a legacy of British imperialism (Arondekar 2009). The ground rules and markers of sexual modernity are a moving target, especially for the non-Western racialised and sexualised other and also for subaltern others within the West. The local and global other can never hope to approximate the dominant Western ideals of sexual normality, for the terms of sexual normality are constantly being rescripted to police entries into the ranks of the Western hegemony.

ACCESS TO ABORTION

When we bring in the politics and discourse around women's reproductive rights, which include access to abortion (in some instances also contraception-see, for example the Hobby Lobby case in the US)[2] the incoherence and fault lines within the sexual landscape, both locally and globally, become inescapably apparent. At this point in time, while male homosexuality tied to pleasure is acquiring greater acceptance, female sexuality for pleasure divorced from reproduction, is regressing. Savita Halappanavar, a woman of Indian origin, died in Ireland in 2012 from a miscarriage that needed medical attention and called for medical termination of her pregnancy.

However, since abortions were and continue to be illegal in Ireland, Savita Halappanavar died rather than get the necessary medical treatment (Pogatchnik 2013). This is seldom referenced in the same context as the celebration of Ireland's "progressive" referendum on gay marriage.

Within the US, in Indiana, Bei-Bei Shuai, a woman of Chinese descent, and a woman of Indian descent, Purvi Patel, were both imprisoned on grounds of obtaining illegal abortions (Tambe 2015). In 2011, Arizona legislators passed the Susan B Anthony and Frederick Douglass Prenatal Nondiscrimination Bill (H R 3541).[3] Even while the bill was named after a well-known US feminist suffrage leader and an African-American abolitionist, it was deeply misogynistic and racist. In criminalising race and sex-selective abortions, the bill placed the onus on women and their providers to prove that their decision for termination of the pregnancy was race and sex neutral. Among others, this bill was aimed at women of Indian and Chinese descent.[4] What we see in this one instance is an absurdly self-serving racist reading of the local in the global. However, this act was not an isolated instance of targeting women of colour. A similar, racist, framing of women of colour as reproductively irre-sponsible and sexually degenerate, marked anti-abortion poster campaigns in New York in 2011. A large billboard in Soho, New York proclaimed, "the most dangerous place for an African-American is in the womb" (Daily Mail 2011).[5] Not surprisingly, given the political orientation of most anti-abortion groups, the message of the poster completely ignored the routine police violence that targets African-Americans on the streets of New York, as elsewhere in the US.

In purporting to advocate for sex and race equality, the Arizona bill placed additional burden of proof on marginalised women of colour, further restricting their access to reproductive health services. While sex-selection abortion is a phenomenon plaguing some communities in India and China, the motivations that lead women and/or their families to seek sex-selection abortions need to be understood within context specific patriarchal structures and cultural scripts.[6] To assume that these structural and discursive frameworks travel in untroubled or uncontested ways into and among diasporic communities, is too simplistic a reading of migrant communities and their cultural negotiations in the host countries. In the instance of the Arizona bill, the underlying assumption is racist in the way it represents immigrant women and their communities. What seems to be at work is the politics of local racist misogyny drawing upon a distant global practice in order to service its sexual surveillance of reproductive bodies, especially those of immigrant women of colour.

READING DIFFERENTLY

A possible way forward from the contemporary impasse on the debate about abortion in the US might be to examine an alternative feminist framing of the issue from a different spatial location, such as India. Reading Indian feminist interventions on abortion and reproductive rights at once highlights the provinciality of the US debate, allowing for recognition of the limits of the current articulations. Some Indian feminists are proposing that women's right to abortion be defended even when guided by the daughter-aversion mindset of sex-selection termination. Recognising the predominantly patriarchal son-preference socio-cultural framework within which Indian women make reproductive decisions, one can appreciate the limits of the "choice" discourse based on Western ideal of individualism. Structural and discursive constraints need to be identified in order to grasp the reproductive logics that guide women's local procreative expressions.[7] Women who undergo sex-selection abortions are neither delusional nor suffering from a false-consciousness, instead, they are acutely aware of the power structures within which they live their everyday precarious lives as sexualised procreative subjects.

To create a more just, egalitarian world, it might be productive to continually trouble universals and to take on the task of prudently unpacking local histories. This approach might, hopefully, allow for a greater appreciation of multiple sexual and procreative practices and theorisings-both spatially and temporally. A new universalist notion of "homophobia" is being deployed to judge, and find wanting, other cultures and groups. This already extends to imposing economic sanctions. There is, in this attempt to universalise Western sexual modernity, something uncannily similar to the ways in which another universal (read Western-parochial) of "women's freedom" was deployed to justify military interventions in the Islamic world. While equality of rights for all, including gay people, is to be applauded, there are dangers when the cultural productions of a small (albeit powerful) part of the world are used to dictate the social and cultural landscape of the rest of the world. We need to work to "provincialise" these universals through insisting on the ways in which local specificities challenge discourses of universal rights.

For instance, in terms of the abortion debate, a possible way forward from the otherwise paralysing dichotomous framing within the US might be to look at an alternative framing of the issue in another global setting, such as India. In India, instead of simply condemning women who undergo sex-selection abortions, some feminists illuminate the patriarchal and misogynistic cultural contexts within which women live their day to day lives. Only by recognising women as reproductive subjects who make decisions within specific material and discursive contexts, can we begin to undo the myth that represents women as unfettered and free-floating liberal subjects shaped by false discourses of choice and individualism. In both the debates on gay marriage and abortion, sexual fault lines need to be recognised as cultural constructs underwritten by complex workings of power which differentially legitimise and delegitimatise sexual and reproductive expressions along intersecting structures of race, class, gender, sexual orientation, religion and nation-locally and globally.

1. How does the author make the case that US abortion restrictions specifically target women of color? Do you agree? Why or why not?

2. The author claims that sex-selective abortion in India illustrates how factors other than individual choice affect women's reproductive rights globally. How can this knowledge illuminate our understanding of the abortion debate in the United States?

"ETHICISTS GENERALLY AGREE: THE PRO-LIFE ARGUMENTS ARE WORTHLESS," JOHN G. MESSERLY, FROM *REASON AND MEANING*, MAY 17, 2016

Abortion continues to make political news, but a question rarely asked by politicians or other interlocutors is: what do professional ethicists think about abortion? If ethicists have reached a consensus about the morality or immorality of abortion, surely their conclusions should be important. And, as a professional ethicist myself, I can tell you that among ethicists it is exceedingly rare to find defenders of the view that abortion is murder. In fact, support for this anti-abortion position, to the extent it exists at all, comes almost exclusively from the small percentage of philosophers who are theists. Yet few seem to take notice of this fact.

To support the claim that the vast majority of ethicists don't favor the pro-life position, consider the disclaimer that appears in the most celebrated anti-abortion piece in the philosophical ethics literature, Don Marquis' "Why Abortion Is Immoral." Marquis begins:

> The view that abortion is, with rare exceptions, seriously immoral has received little support in the recent philosophical literature. No doubt most philosophers affiliated with secular institutions of higher education believe that the anti-abortion position is either a symptom of irrational religious dogma or a conclusion generated by seriously confused philosophical argument.

Marquis concedes that abortion isn't considered immoral according to most ethicists, but why is this? Perhaps professional ethicists, who are typically non-religious philosophers, find nothing morally objectionable about abortion because they aren't religious. In other words, if they were devout they would recognize abortion as a moral abomination. But we could easily turn this around. Perhaps religiously oriented ethicists oppose abortion because they are religious. In other words, if there weren't devout they would see that abortion isn't morally problematic. So both religious and secular ethicists could claim that the other side prejudges the case.

However, it is definitely not the case that secular ethicists care less about life or morality than religious ethicists. Consider that virtually all moral philosophers believe that murder, theft, torture, and lying are immoral because cogent arguments such prohibitions. Oftentimes there is little difference between the views of religious and secular ethicists. Moreover, when there is disagreement among the two groups, perhaps the secular philosophers are actually ahead of the ethical curve with their acceptance of things like abortion, homosexuality, and certain forms of euthanasia.

How then do we adjudicate disputes in the moral realm when ethicists, like ordinary people, start with different assumptions? The key to answering this question is to emphasize reason and argument, the hallmarks of doing philosophical ethics. Both secular and religious individuals can participate in a forum of rational discourse to resolve their disputes. In fact, natural law moral theory—the dominant ethical theory throughout the history of Christianity—claims that moral laws are reasonable, which means that what is right is supported by the best rational arguments. Natural law theorists argue that by exercising the human reason their God has given them, they can understand what is right and wrong. Thus, secular and religious philosophers work in the same arena, one where moral truths are those supported by the best reasons.

That ethicists emphasize rational discourse may be counter-intuitive in a society dominated by appeals to emotion, prejudice, faith, and group loyalty. But ethicists, secular and religious alike, try to impartially examine the arguments for and against moral propositions in order to determine where the weight of reason lies in the matter. Ethicists may not be perfect umpires, and the truth about moral matters is often difficult to tease out, but ethicists are trained to be impartial and thorough when analyzing arguments. Some are better at this than others, but when a significant majority agrees, it is probably because some arguments really are stronger than others.

Now you might wonder what make ethicists better able to adjudicate between good and bad arguments than ordinary people. The answer is that professional ethicists are schooled in logic and the critical thinking skills demanded by those who carefully and conscientiously examine arguments. They are also trained in the more abstract fields of meta-ethics, which considers the meaning of moral terms and concepts, as well as in ethical theory, which considers norms, standards, or criteria for moral conduct. Moreover, they are familiar with the best philosophical arguments that have been advanced for and against moral propositions. So they are in a good position to reject arguments that influence those unfamiliar with positions that oppose their favored ones.

All this education doesn't mean that the majority of ethicists are right, so individuals who disagree with them may choose to follow their own conscience. But if the vast majority of ethicists agree about an ethics issue, we should take notice. It might be that the reasons you give for your fervently held moral beliefs don't stand up to critical scrutiny. Perhaps they can't be rationally defended as well as those reached after conscientious, informed, and impartial analysis. This doesn't mean that you should ignore your conscience and accept expert opinion, but if you are serious about a moral problem you should want to know the views of those who have thoroughly studied the issue.

At this point you might object that there are no moral experts because ethics is relative to an individual's opinions or emotions. You might say that the experts have their opinion and you have yours, and that's the end of it. Perhaps behaviors in the moral realm are just like carrots—some people like them and some don't. This theory is called personal moral relativism. However, not only do most ethicists reject moral relativism, so must pro-lifers. After all, pro-lifers [do not] think that the moral prohibition against abortion is relative; they think its absolute. They believe that there are good reasons why abortion is immoral that any rational person should accept. However these reasons must be evaluated to see if they are really good ones; to see if they convince other knowledgeable persons. Yet so far, the pro-life arguments haven't persuaded many ethicists.

Lacking good reasons or armed with weak ones, many will object that their moral beliefs derive from their God. To base your ethical views on Gods you would need to know: 1) if Gods exists; 2) if they are good; 3) if they issue good commands; 4) how to find the commands; and 5) the proper version and translation of the holy books issuing commands, or the right interpretation of a revelation of the commands, or the legitimacy of a church authority issuing commands. Needless to say, it is hard, if not impossible, to know any of this.

Consider just the interpretation problem. When does a seemingly straightforward command from a holy book like, "thou shalt not kill," apply? In self defense? In war? Always? And to whom does it apply? To non-human animals? Intelligent aliens? Serial killers? All living things? The unborn? The brain dead? Religious commands such as "don't kill," "honor thy parents," and "don't commit adultery" are ambiguous. Difficulties also arise if we hear voices commanding us, or if we accept an institution's authority. Why trust the voices in our heads, or institutional authorities?

For the sake of argument though, let's assume: that there are Gods; that you know the true one; that your God issues good commands; that you have access to them because you have found the right book or church, or had the right vision, or heard the right voices; and that you interpret and understand the command correctly—even if they came from a book that has been translated from one language to another over thousands of years or from a long ago revelation. It is unlikely that you are correct about all this, but for the sake of the argument let's say that you are. Even in that case most philosophers would argue that you can't base ethics on your God.

To understand why you can't base ethics on Gods consider the question: what is the relationship between the Gods and their commands? A classic formulation of this relationship is called the divine-command theory.

According to divine command theory, things are right or wrong simply because the Gods command or forbid them. There is nothing more to morality than this. It's like a parent who says to a child: it's right because I say so. To see how this formulation of the relationship fails, consider a famous philosophical conundrum: "Are things right because the Gods command them, or do the Gods command them because they are right?"

If things are right simply because the Gods command them, then their commands are arbitrary. In that case the Gods could have made their commandments backwards! If divine fiat is enough to make something right, then the Gods could have commanded us to kill, lie, cheat, steal and commit adultery, and those behaviors would then be moral. But the Gods can't make something right, if it's wrong. The Gods can't make torturing children morally acceptable simply by divine decree, and that is the main reason why most Christian theologians reject divine command theory.

On the other hand, if the Gods command things because they are right, then there are reasons for the God's commands. On this view the Gods, in their infinite wisdom and benevolence, command things because they see certain commands as good for us. But if this is the case, then there is some standard, norm or criteria by which good or bad are measured which is independent of the Gods. Thus all us, religious and secular alike, should be looking for the reasons that certain behaviors should be condemned or praised. Even the thoughtful believer should engage in philosophical ethics.

So either the Gods commands are without reason and therefore arbitrary, or they are rational according to some standard. This standard—say that we would all be better off—is thus the reason we should be moral and that reason, not the Gods' authority, is what makes something right or wrong. The same is true for a supposedly authoritative book. Something isn't wrong simply because a book says so. There must be a reason that something is right or wrong, and if there isn't, then the book has no moral authority on the matter.

At this point the believer might object that the Gods have reasons for their commands, but we can't know them. Yet if the ways of the Gods are really mysterious to us, what's the point of religion? If you can't know anything about the Gods or their commands, then why follow those commands, why have religion at all, why listen to the priest or preacher? If it's all a mystery, we should remain silent or become mystics.

In response the religious may say that, even though they don't know the reason for their God's commands, they must oppose abortion because of the inerrancy of their sacred scriptures or church tradition. They might say that since the Bible and their church oppose abortion, that's good enough for them, despite what moral philosophers say. But in fact neither church authority nor Christian scripture unequivocally oppose abortion.

As for scriptures, they don't generally offer specific moral guidance. Moreover, most ancient scriptures survived as oral traditions before being written down; they have been translated multiple times; they are open to multiple interpretations; and they don't discuss many contemporary moral issues. Furthermore, the issue of abortion doesn't arise in the Christian scriptures except tangentially. There are a few Biblical passages quoted by conservatives to support the anti-abortion position, the most well-known is in Jeremiah: "Before I formed you in the womb I knew you, and before you were born I consecrated you." But, as anyone who has examined this passage knows, the sanctity of fetal life isn't being discussed here. Rather, Jeremiah is asserting his authority as a prophet. This is a classic example of seeking support in holy books for a position you already hold.

Many other Biblical passages point to the more liberal view of abortion. Three times in the Bible (Genesis 38:24; Leviticus 21:9; Deuteronomy 22:20–21) the death penalty is recommended for women who have sex out-of-wedlock, even though killing the women would kill their fetuses. In Exodus 21 God prescribes death as the penalty for murder, whereas the penalty for causing a woman to miscarry is a fine. In the Old Testament the fetus doesn't seem to have personhood status, and the New Testament says nothing about abortion at all. There simply isn't a strong scriptural tradition in Christianity against abortion.

There also is no strong church tradition against abortion. It is true that the Catholic Church has held for centuries that activities like contraception and abortion which interrupt natural processes are immoral. Yet, while most pro-lifers don't consider those distributing birth control to be murderers, the Catholic Church and others do take the extreme view that abortion is murder. Where does such a strong condemnation come from? The history of the Catholic view isn't clear on the issue, but in the 13th century the philosopher Thomas Aquinas argued that the soul enters the body when the zygote has a human shape. Gradually other Christian theologians came to believe that the soul enters the body a few days after conception, although we don't exactly know why they believed this. But, given what we now know about fetal development, if the Catholic Church's position remained consistent with the views of Aquinas, they should say that the soul doesn't enter the zygote for at least a month or two after conception. (Note also that there is no moment of conception, despite popular belief to the contrary.)

Thus the anti-abortion position doesn't clearly follow from either scripture or church tradition. Instead what happens is that people already have moral views, and they then look to their religion for support. In other words, moral convictions aren't usually derived from scripture or church tradition so much as superimposed on them. (For example, Christians used the Bible to both support and oppose slavery in the period before the American Civil War.) But even if the pro-life position did follow from a religious tradition, that would only be relevant for religious believers. For the rest of us, and for many religious believers too, the best way to adjudicate our disputes without resorting to violence is to conscientiously examine the arguments for and against moral propositions by shining the light of reason upon them.

It also clearly follows that religious believers have no right to impose their views upon the rest of us. We live in a morally pluralistic society where, informed by the ethos of the Enlightenment, we should reject attempts to impose theocracy. We should allow people to follow their conscience in moral matters—you can drink alcohol—as long as others aren't harmed—you shouldn't drink and drive. In philosophy of law, this is known as the harm principle. If rational argumentation supported the view that the zygote is a full person, then we might have reason to outlaw abortion, inasmuch as abortion would harm another person. (I say might because the fact that something is a person doesn't necessarily imply that's it wrong to kill it, as defenders of war, self-defense and capital punishment maintain.)

But for now the received view among ethicists is that the pro-life arguments fail, primarily because the fetus satisfies few if any of the necessary and sufficient conditions for personhood. The impartial view, backed by contemporary biology and philosophical argumentation, is that a zygote is a potential person. That doesn't mean it has no moral significance, but it does mean that it has less significance than an actual person. An acorn may become an oak tree, but an oak tree it is not. You may believe that your God puts souls into newly fertilized eggs, thereby granting them full personhood, but that is a religious belief not grounded in science or philosophical ethics.

As for American politics and abortion, no doubt much of the anti-abortion rhetoric in American society comes from a punitive, puritanical desire to punish people for having sex. Moreover, many are hypocritical on the issue, simultaneously opposing abortion as well as the only proven ways of reducing it—good sex education and readily available birth control. As for many (if not most) politicians, their public opposition is hypocritical and self-interested. Generally they don't care about the issue—they care about the power and wealth derived from politics—but they feign concern by throwing red meat to their constituencies. They use the issue as a ploy to garner support from the unsuspecting. These politicians may be pro-birth, but they aren't generally pro-life, as evidenced by their opposition to policies that would support the things that children need most after birth like education, health-care, and economic opportunities. But what politicians and many ordinary people clearly don't care about is whether their fanatical anti-abortion position is based in rational argumentation.

1. Is the schism between religious belief and philosophy responsible for disagreement on abortion in your opinion? Or is it more an issue of social pressure or political allegiance?

2. Do you agree with the author's assessment that "much of the anti-abortion rhetoric in American society comes from a punitive, puritanical desire to punish people for having sex"?

CHAPTER 2

WHAT THE GOVERNMENT AND POLITICIANS SAY

*R*oe v. *Wade* may be the law of the land, but abortion opponents continue efforts to chip away at this historic ruling. On the federal level, HR 36, otherwise known as the Pain-Capable Unborn Child Protection Act, seeks to outlaw abortion after twenty weeks of pregnancy. It is currently in effect in fourteen states. A slew of additional measures against abortion on the state level were passed in the wake of 2014 Republican victories in two-thirds of the state legislatures. Newly emboldened, lawmakers redoubled their efforts with a vengeance, passing 231 new laws restricting access to abortion in 2015.

This chapter examines some of the legal and rhetorical strategies abortion opponents are using to enact new restrictions. As the saying goes, "the devil is in the details"; pro-life legislators have trained their sights on these very details, passing laws that, among other restrictions, impose long waiting periods on women seeking abortions, target the physical facilities of abortion providers, and allow doctors to opt out of abortions for reasons of conscience even if the health of the mother is in danger.

A common feature of much recent anti-abortion legislation is the masking of potentially dangerous restrictions with language about the health of the mother. For example, in Texas, Targeted Regulation of Abortion Providers (TRAP) laws required facilities providing abortions to have surgical-grade operating facilities, even if to only administer medically induced abortions. Naturally, few clinics could afford this expensive equipment, and most were forced to shut down. In Ohio, so-called transfer laws required an abortion clinic to have admitting privileges at a nearby hospital to remain in operation. In an increasingly conservative climate, few hospitals voluntarily signed such agreements. Ironically, these impediments to a safe abortion risk jeopardizing the health of the mother. The functional result of these laws is reduced access to abortion.

Another problem is a lack of abortion training for future doctors due to fiscal pressures and potential disputes with faith-based hospitals. Groups such as Medical Students for Choice fill in this gap. Founder Jody Steinauer here recounts that when she completed her residency in obstetrics and gynecology, only 12 percent of such programs taught the abortion procedure, a staggeringly low number given that 1.2 million abortions are performed annually,

Pro-choice advocates have some positive news. According to a recent Supreme Court decision, Texas's TRAP laws were said to create an "onerous burden" on abortion, and were therefore deemed unconstitutional. Although this is encouraging, the continued struggle to prevent further rollbacks on *Roe* prevents the expanding of reproductive health care services to all women, regardless of race, class, or other factors.

"7 REPRODUCTIVE RIGHTS ISSUES TO WATCH IN 2015," BY NINA MARTIN, FROM *PROPUBLICA*, JANUARY 16, 2015

To say abortion opponents are feeling fired up in 2015 would be a massive understatement. In their first week back at work, congressional Republicans introduced a sweeping prohibition on abortions after 20 weeks of pregnancy (H.R. 36, the Pain-Capable Unborn Child Protection Act), as well as bills that would ban sex-selective abortions, target funding for groups like Planned Parenthood, require abortion providers to have hospital admitting privileges, and let doctors and nurses opt out of providing abortion care, even in emergencies. In the states, where the 2014 elections gave Republicans control of two-thirds of state legislative chambers, incoming lawmakers also have supersized their abortion agendas. But abortion is just one issue on the minds of activists focused on reproductive rights. There's also birth control, conscience clauses and personhood. Here are seven key trends and themes to watch for this year.

1. A NEW WAVE OF ABORTION RESTRICTIONS

Despite the GOP-controlled Congress, a Democrat in the White House means that many of the most significant battles over abortion will continue to take place in state-houses and courtrooms, not on Capitol Hill.

Expect to see a torrent of 20-week bans like the one Congress has proposed (13 states already have similar laws on the books). These bills are being advanced by groups like the Susan B. Anthony List; a report by the group's research arm, the Charlotte Lozier Institute, recently noted that in most countries where abortion is legal, the procedure is limited to early pregnancy. "The U.S. is in very rare and unsavory company in allowing abortion [after 20 weeks]," Lozier's president, Chuck Donovan, said in an interview, pointing to China and North Korea as two other outliers. Even if President Obama ends up vetoing some version of the 20-week ban, Donovan said, "It could actually heighten awareness of the issue."

In a few states, lawmakers are expected to dust off retro theories (a Missouri bill, for example, would require women to get permission from the fetus's father to have an abortion, an idea ruled unconstitutional in 1992). An Indiana bill that would make it illegal for doctors to perform an abortion based on a fetal abnormality such as Down syndrome echoes abortion foes' efforts in Ohio, North Dakota and elsewhere to position themselves as protectors of the disabled.

Other bills will be aimed at tightening abortion restrictions already in place—lengthening waiting periods to 72 hours, for example, and making it harder for teens to use judicial bypass procedures to obtain an abortion without their parents' permission. (A new Alabama law gives the fetus in such cases its own attorney.) "It's possibly an easier lift to amend an existing law," said Elizabeth Nash, a senior policy associate at the Guttmacher Institute. "It's smart."

Also on the horizon: a likely clampdown on medical abortions (those induced by drugs). Meanwhile, all sides will be watching to see how the 5th Circuit Court of Appeals, and eventually the U.S. Supreme Court, deals with Texas restrictions known as TRAP, or Targeted Regulation of Abortion Providers, laws—rules that purportedly make clinics, and abortion, safer but could shutter most of the clinics in that state. A key question: how many clinics have to shut down before the TRAP laws create an "undue burden" on women's right to abortion, effectively rendering *Roe v. Wade* moot?

2. THE RISE OF RELIGIOUS EXEMPTIONS

This trend has its roots in two recent Supreme Court decisions: last June's *Hobby Lobby* ruling and the 2013 *Windsor* case upholding gay marriage.

At the center of *Hobby Lobby* was the federal Religious Freedom Restoration Act of 1993, which says that the government can only "substantially burden" the exercise of religion if it has a "compelling state interest." The Supreme Court's precedent-shattering interpretation—that RFRA applied to closely held companies like the retailer Hobby Lobby, whose owners objected to the Affordable Care Act's contraception mandate on religious grounds—was "a minefield," Justice Ruth Bader Ginsburg warned.

And sure enough, the past six months have brought an explosion in religious-exemption challenges involving everyone and everything from a Missouri lawmaker who didn't want his teenage daughters to have access to birth control to Native Americans battling federal rules that make it illegal to possess the feathers of certain types of endangered eagles without a permit. (The feathers are used in religious ceremonies.)

Some state lawmakers, meanwhile, have taken inspiration from the *Hobby Lobby* decision to fight back against the stunning gains of the marriage equality movement since *Windsor.* They have introduced a deluge of RFRA-type bills that would allow business owners, local government officials, and health care professionals to refuse to provide services to gay people—rent a banquet hall, issue a marriage license, perform in vitro fertilization—that violate their religious beliefs. Same-sex marriage may be the immediate target, but state RFRAs would likely have a much broader impact, said Katherine Franke, co-director of the Center for Gender and Sexuality Law at Columbia, granting "a kind of blanket indemnity from compliance with all sorts of otherwise applicable laws." That could erode not just reproductive and gender rights but eventually, Franke said, protections against race discrimination as well. Catholic hospitals—engaged in high-profile battles with the ACLU in Michigan and elsewhere over limits on reproductive care—would also benefit.

3. CONSCIENCE CLAUSES FOR NON-RELIGIOUS GROUPS

Back in Washington, anti-abortion groups have been working to extend religious-type "conscience" exemptions to non-religious organizations—starting with themselves.

Last summer, March for Life—the organization behind the demonstrations in front of the Supreme Court every January 22 on the anniversary of *Roe v. Wade*—filed a lawsuit demanding an exemption from the ACA's contraception mandate, arguing that it "fundamentally violates" the group's core principles.

"Because they aren't a religious organization, they can't claim an exemption under RFRA," said Casey Mattox, senior counsel at Alliance Defending Freedom, the conservative legal powerhouse that brought the suit. The same is true for many other anti-abortion organizations. "We think we have a conscience claim beyond religious belief," the Lozier Institute's Donovan said. Their argument: Denying abortion opponents the same exemption given to religious groups violates their constitutional right to equal protection.

4. BATTLES OVER CONTRACEPTION

One of the most striking aspects of the March for Life suit is its assertion that birth control—the hormonal kind, as well as intrauterine devices—are "abortifacients" (meaning they cause abortions). Indeed, the Lozier Institute published a paper last year arguing that emergency contraception is essentially no different from abortion because it purportedly prevents implantation of a fertilized egg. (Women's groups and their allies say the scientific evidence proves otherwise.)

The arguments are part of a larger strategy that reproductive rights advocates say has been gaining strength in recent years, with a major boost from *Hobby Lobby*. "Birth control is very much in the [anti-abortion] movement's cross-hairs," Guttmacher policy researcher Joerg Dreweke wrote in a recent analysis, "and antiabortion advocates are working to stigmatize contraception by blurring the lines between contraception and abortion."

The U.S. Catholic bishops, meanwhile, also are also likely to zero in on birth control and sterilizations as they begin the process of revising their rules governing Catholic health care.

5. A REVAMPED PERSONHOOD PLAYBOOK

Last November was supposed to be a turning point for the personhood movement, which argues that establishing the legal rights of "pre-born humans" is the key to overturning *Roe*. And the 2014 election was a turning point —but not in the way supporters had hoped. A "human life amendment" to North Dakota's constitution that had been expected to win overwhelming approval ended up being trounced at the polls; ditto for a ballot measure in Colorado. The election results triggered what Gualberto Garcia Jones, national policy director for the National Personhood Alliance, called "an existential crisis" for the movement. In a tough-talking post-election analysis on LifeSite News, he warned, "[A] lot has to change."

One sign of change is the emergence of NPA itself. Instead of the statewide ballot measures favored by Personhood USA, the heretofore leader of the movement, NPA will promote what Garcia Jones called "asymmetrical tactics ... engaging the enemy in municipalities and counties that we know we control." Daniel Becker, NPA's Georgia-based president, said he's looking for "opportunities to personalize the child in the womb" via fetal rights legislation on everything from inheritance to adoption. He also favors statutes like those in Alabama and Tennessee that target drug use during pregnancy.

A key goal, Becker said, is "to create tension in the law" that would require courts—and eventually the U.S. Supreme Court—to act. Part of that strategy, he added, is to identify potentially sympathetic judges like the ones on the Alabama Supreme Court (see ProPublica's story about one of those justices here) *[Editor's note: This article can be found at https://www.propublica.org/article/this-alabama-judge-has-figured-out-how-to-dismantle-roe-v-wade].*

As the personhood movement regroups, expect reproductive rights organizations to start talking more about personhood, too—the personhood of the mother-to-be.

"When you look at [these laws] collectively, you cannot miss the fact that people with a capacity for pregnancy have a second-class status in this country," said Lynn Paltrow, executive director of National Advocates for Pregnant Women, which fights measures like the ones Becker supports "They haven't achieved full personhood. That is what the battle really is."

6. A BROADER AGENDA FOR REPRODUCTIVE RIGHTS ACTIVISTS

For years, protecting *Roe v. Wade* has been the almost singular focus of reproductive rights advocates. But more recently, many have become convinced that narrow focus could spell doom. The ideological divide over "choice" vs. "life" "doesn't fit the reality of many families," said Denicia Cadena of the New Mexico group Young Women United. In many parts of the country, even among those who favor abortion rights, abortion is a topic that "stops conversations," said Monica Simpson, executive director of Sister Song, which focuses on the South. "It shuts people down."

The soul-searching—some of it painfully public—has led to a shift that will become more evident in 2015.

Advocates in a number of states are focusing on proactive bills that aim to improve the lives of women and children by raising the minimum wage, requiring paid sick leave, strengthening protections against pregnancy discrimination, and pressing for education and criminal justice reforms. More groups are talking about the intersection between LGBT and reproductive issues, often in the context of transgender health. There is, said Simpson, less talk about "choice" and more about "justice."

Meanwhile, groups such as the recently formed CoreAlign are working with allies in conservative areas to develop a 30-year strategic plan that might reframe reproductive rights issues and transform public opinion. One part of the plan: Training a new generation of leaders—many from communities of color—who can see it through. Andrea Miller, president of the National Institute for Reproductive Health, a think tank that supports state activists, pointed out that anti-abortion groups did much the same thing, with considerable success. "They started local. They made a coordinated effort to work their ways into the legislative and political process, and eventually they created a tipping point," Miller said.

Which is not to say that reproductive rights groups are abandoning their core issue. Last year saw the introduction of more new state laws protecting abortion than at any time since 1990.

7. THE CALIFORNIA EXCEPTION

For reproductive rights advocates, California has been one of the few bright spots in recent years. In 2013, for example, the state passed a law that allowed trained non-doctors to perform first-trimester abortions—the largest expansion of abortion access in the U.S. in a decade. Researchers affiliated with the University of California–San Francisco are expected to publish more studies on abortion safety—as well as the real-world consequences of preventing women who want abortions from having them. This research has been influential well beyond the state's borders.

Which is one reason anti-abortion groups are paying such close attention to the next big California case on the horizon: A determination by insurance regulators last year that every health plan in the state must cover all maternity-related services, including abortion—even plans offered by Catholic schools and hospitals. Americans Defending Freedom has filed a complaint with the U.S. Department of Health and Human Services, and religious and anti-abortion groups are girding for an epic battle.

1. How would you describe the state of reproductive rights in 2015? To what degree were they jeopardized by these many new attacks?

2. The article notes that some reproductive rights activists prefer to reframe "choice" as "justice." What do you think of this shift?

"THE LANDSCAPE OF STATE ANTI-ABORTION LEGISLATION," BY RACHEL SUSSMAN, FROM *THE COLUMBIA JOURNAL OF GENDER AND LAW*, 2015

Rachel Sussman: Thanks, everybody, for having me. I'm thrilled to be here. I spend most of my time reading bills that intend to restrict access to reproductive healthcare, and taking a break from that, stepping back and hearing from others in this environment, is really important. So I'm thrilled to be here, thank you.

To start, I'll make a quick note about Planned Parenthood. I think we exist in a unique space with regard to advocacy. We are a healthcare provider, so we have hundreds of health centers across the country. One in five women in the United States will visit a Planned Parenthood at some point in her life.[1] So our advocacy and the way we move forward, whether through litigation or public policy and legislation, first and foremost focuses on our patients and how we can serve them best.

So that gives us a unique platform. It also can be challenging because not only are we advocating for our patients, but often we must advocate for ourselves as a service provider in order to keep our doors open.

I will focus on the legislative landscape for reproductive health issues. With the change in control of state legislatures and governors' offices in the 2010 elections came a complete onslaught of efforts to restrict reproductive health services. The floodgates opened.

Arizona is a good example. When Janet Napolitano was in office as governor, she was busy. Veto, veto, veto, veto, right? She had to veto a lot of bad bills. But as soon as she left in 2010, all of the restrictions around reproductive health care services started passing and getting signed.[2] There were hundreds and hundreds of bills. Tracking them alone is a challenge. So to then try to stop them through advocacy in such hostile environments can be very difficult.

Because the environment is so hostile, one tactic that Planned Parenthood and other advocacy organizations has used is simply elevating the fact that this barrage of restrictions is happening. We did this by saying at a fundamental level, our opposition's main goal is trying to chip away at *Roe v. Wade* through both public policy and public opinion. And so this opening of the floodgates and moving all of these bills represents their effort of chipping away in earnest.

Historically, we had seen many bills that attempted to create barriers for women trying to access abortion. So, for example, we have seen bills that instituted a 24-hour waiting period, or requirements that women go through counseling and hear information that either isn't true or is biased.

What I think switched in 2010--and Bebe Anderson alluded to this in talking about the opposition's efforts to push the frame of keeping women safe[3]--is they started to get into the business of actually regulating health-care. And through these regulations, which I'm going to talk about in a minute, they were in effect trying to shut down health centers. The regulations may be impossible to comply with, or have absolutely no impact in terms of actual medical safety and therefore may be inappropriate to comply with, or force doctors to actually provide bad medicine.

Right now there are five main categories of bills in my world. The restrictions I was just mentioning that attempt to regulate and shut down health centers are in a broader rubric of what I call "TRAP" bills. "TRAP" stands for Targeted Restrictions on Abortion Providers. These are all sorts of laws that seek to regulate the physical building of a health center or create staffing requirements. And many of these bills literally would require health centers to build hospital-style operating rooms even in a health center that only offers medication abortion. So a woman may decide to experience the abortion through medica-tion and the provider is just handing her the pills, yet they have to be in an operating room. Right? So on its face, it sounds ridiculous.

The challenge is the framing--most people want everyone to have the best and safest healthcare. Part of our challenge is that the fight over regulation of health-care is happening at a time where we also have a national conversation about access to healthcare and there are a lot of concerns that people generally have in regards to how they're experiencing their healthcare. So when

all of a sudden people are talking about more regula-
tion--making it safer, making it better--it reassures those
anxieties. That is the environment we have to work in,
which is extremely challenging.

We are still forging forward, and I think Texas is a
great example of people really seeing what these bills
are intended to do, and seeing that the result is restricted
access.[4] On a fundamental level, health centers close
down, and women have less access to care. And when
women have less access to care, they are forced to seek
methods that are less safe. It actually goes against what
the opposition is proposing, right? The story can be told.
But it's a long story, and sometimes in the public sphere
or in the media, you don't have a really long time to tell it.

The other area where we're seeing restrictions
and a doubling down on them is around actual banning
of abortions. In the past couple of years, states have
tried to ban abortion at six weeks, twelve weeks.[5] There's
been an escalation of banning abortion at twenty weeks,
which has been through the courts in some states.[6] But
for many women who are seeking abortion at that point
in pregnancy, it is usually due to a complication or something going wrong with the pregnancy. And even in that
context, it's a hard fight. Getting women to come forward,
to tell their story, in some ways--and I know we're going to
get to this--has been far more challenging in the context
of access to abortion than I think it has been for the gay
rights community and marriage.

I know I'm running low on time so I will just mention
a few other categories of restrictions. We are seeing an
escalation of waiting periods. We no longer see twenty-
four-hour waiting periods; we're seeing forty-eight-hour

and seventy-two-hour waiting periods.[7] It's sad when you say, "Oh, I wish I were seeing twenty-four-hour waiting periods." In some states there are actually seventy-two-hour waiting periods on the books. And for women who have to arrange childcare and travel, seventy-two hours can easily turn into a week.

And then I think we're going to get to talk about this more later, so I will just mention the refusal context. For years we have seen laws on the books that either are expansions of Religious Freedom Restoration Acts or are just straight-up refusal laws that allow individuals or entities to refuse to provide reproductive health care services.[8] I think these barriers will continue to exist, and I think we'll hopefully have collaboration on fighting it as we move forward.

Here, the panel turned to questions about the generational aspect of the work, movement priorities, and connections across reproductive rights and marriage equality work.

Question 1: One of the things that I'm really interested in is the generational aspect of this work. Because while I think that there is a lot of similarity between LGBT rights and reproductive rights, there's a huge difference in terms of how the younger generation is seeing these issues. Because one of the biggest differences is that young people are seriously in favor of looking at sexuality and sexual orientation in an entirely different way from the way previous generations did. But that's not the case around abortion. In fact, what you're seeing is the younger generation getting more and more conservative around the issue of abortion. And I think that that's one of the big differences. So my question really is to Jessica around how you're having a values debate with a much younger generation that sees abortion very differently.

Question 2: On this question of what's next, what do you all hope are the priorities in ten years in the reproductive and LGBT rights movements?

Question 3: I have a question for my colleagues in the equality field. So everybody this morning from the choice side has talked about how once we won the federal rights in *Roe v. Wade* they were then subsequently chipped away at. Poor women, minors, lots of other women were denied the right for a couple of decades and still are. And my question for you guys is, have you already been giving some thought to what are your equivalents to a chipping away, because in that case, there's an actual service that can be denied, and so I'm just trying to be thoughtful about that. But I'm curious if you have ideas about that.

Suzanne Goldberg: When you think about the work that you have done, in whichever areas you have focused, how do you see the connections across marriage equality work and LGBT work generally, as well as reproductive rights and freedom work? Some of the disconnections are clear in terms of the challenges that reproductive rights have faced in recent years and the relative successes that marriage equality work has faced. But there are all sorts of disconnections and connections and so I welcome you all to speak about anything you like.

Rachel Sussman: I wanted to talk a little bit about the public opinion pieces raised. One of the fundamental things that on a daily basis slightly confuses me is that an overwhelming majority of the public supports Roe v. Wade.[9] They support abortion staying safe and legal, and actually, those numbers don't really shift with millennial. I do completely agree that our dialogue and the way we've talked about either access to abortion or just about making private medical decisions has to change. And I think shifting how we talk to younger people and how we engage them is something that the reproductive health community is actively focused on.

But the reality is, the people are there. They generally support access to abortion. And so why is that not always translating? And I think there have been snippets of moments, like we've seen in Texas and in North Carolina, where people are so frustrated that they come out and actively oppose and push back against restrictions. But there are a ton of places where that's not happening. And I think the outrage that we just saw in Arizona around refusal for the LGBT community doesn't have an equivalent in the reproductive rights community.[10] John McCain isn't coming out and saying these abortion restrictions are wrong. Right? It is still a very polarizing conversation to the extent that it's hard to get folks to come out and honestly say what they believe. I mean, I just strongly believe there are a lot of people out there, including elected officials, who basically support *Roe* and access to abortion and who do not come out and stand up and fight for it. And that is, I think, a challenge for our community, because it seems like one party's thing is that they're pushing to show they are different from the other party. But the people's reluctance to show their support for safe and legal abortion is not really changing.

Another example is Mississippi, where they defeated a personhood ballot initiative.[11] I mean, we won in Mississippi. Right? So the fact is that when we're able to engage in a conversation with the public on this issue, when we're able to talk about what it actually means and the impact for women and their families, we win. But frankly, the amount of money that it cost, and the length of time that we had to engage the public for one ballot initiative in Mississippi, is very different from the situation when you're facing an entire legislative session. For example, in Missouri, there are twenty-six bills attempting to restrict reproductive health access just this session.[12] So who are you talking to about what, right? So I think those are some of our challenges.

One similarity that I see is that the group that was pushing the LGBT refusal bill in Arizona was the Center for Arizona Policy. That same group has pushed and passed--I can't even count how many--restrictions on reproductive healthcare in Arizona.[13] So the reality is that our opposition is the same for both LGBT rights and reproductive healthcare, and that could create opportunities for collaboration.

These remarks were presented at the Center for Gender & Sexuality Law's Symposium on Marriage Equality and Reproductive Rights: Lessons Learned and the Road Ahead, held at Columbia Law School on February 28, 2014.

1. How would you characterize the dissonance between the stated and practical purposes of so-called TRAP laws? Why are these so effective at limiting access to abortions, according to the author?

2. Given that the majority of Americans support *Roe v. Wade*, why is the pushback against abortion rights we currently see, for example in Texas, working?

"AS STATES TRY TO CURB ABORTION, FUTURE DOCTORS FIGHT FOR TRAINING," BY HEIDI LANDECKER, FROM *THE CHRONICLE OF HIGHER EDUCATION*, JUNE 21, 2013

By imposing restrictions on abortion clinics, more and more state legislatures are trying to limit *Roe v. Wade*. Now a university medical center has aided that effort, raising questions about whether its actions are in the best interests of medical education and public health.

In April the University of Toledo Medical Center, after criticism from Ohio Right to Life, declined to renew a so-called transfer agreement with one abortion clinic and stopped arranging one with another. The agreements establish that clinics may move a patient to a hospital in an emergency. Without them, a clinic can't operate in Ohio, limiting opportunities for valuable training experience for medical students and residents.

The university's president, Lloyd A. Jacobs, says its hospital will "take patients in our emergency room from anywhere, anytime, from any background, under any circumstance." But seeking "a more neutral position," he wants to free his state institution from transfer agreements with abortion clinics.

No other local hospital will sign the agreements. One clinic, Center for Choice, said last week that it was closing; Capital Care Network will probably close in July, when its agreement with the university expires.

Carolyn Payne, a rising third-year medical student at the University of Toledo and president of its chapter of Medical Students for Choice, says that isn't right. She and about 15 other students volunteered at Center for Choice, working with counselors and a doctor to learn abortion care. She will now have to go to another city—an hour away—to learn this common medical procedure.

Nearly a third of all American women will have an abortion by age 45, according to the Guttmacher Institute, which studies and advocates for reproductive health and rights. Yet lectures and rotations covering abortion are surprisingly scant in medical-school education, especially in the South and Midwest. And if abortion isn't taught in medical schools, a shortage of doctors who perform them will make *Roe v. Wade* irrelevant.

'SHOOT THE ABORTIONIST'

Medical Students for Choice was started 20 years ago by Jody Steinauer, now an associate clinical professor of obstetrics and gynecology at the University of California at San Francisco. In early 1993, she and other medical students across the country received a "jokebook," mailed to their homes, that included "Q: What would you do if you were in a room with Hitler, Mussolini, and an abortionist, and you had a gun with only two bullets? A: Shoot the abortionist twice."

About the same time, Dr. Steinauer learned that only 12 percent of ob-gyn residency programs, where medical-school graduates practice under the tutelage of physicians, were teaching the procedure-a big drop from a decade earlier.

Then, in March 1993, David Gunn, an obstetrician who performed abortions, was shot and killed in Pensacola, Fla. "Of course we have to fight for this," Ms. Steinauer told herself. "How can we let politics and stigma determine what future physicians are learning?"

Taking a year off from medical school, she helped found a nonprofit that would eventually tap into growing numbers of pro-choice students.

Medical Students for Choice now has 159 chapters in the United States and 12 other countries, including Ireland (a rich environment for student activism despite abortion's being illegal there). With 10,000 student members, the group's staff of seven, based in Philadelphia, works with those like Ms. Payne in Toledo—helping draft petitions, get faculty support, and examine legal aspects of the university's decision to end its agreement with the local clinics.

The group, whose motto is "creating tomorrow's abortion providers and pro-choice physicians," also holds two-day training institutes on specific topics, bringing students from all over who apply. It offers a reproductive-health "externship," in which students concerned about gaps in abortion teaching at their own medical schools can spend a month at a school with comprehensive reproductive-health training. And it holds annual family-planning conferences in the United States, Canada, and, this fall, an international meeting in Dublin.

Before the Toledo clinic crisis, Medical Students for Choice was helping Ms. Payne advocate for classroom education about abortion. In May she outlined her strategy in Atlanta, at an MSFC Activist Training Institute, to 20 students from as far away as Newfoundland and California.

She described showing the chair of her school's ob-gyn department what the different hours of lectures were spent on in students' first years—two hours on organ donation, for example, whereas abortion was never discussed. "I made the case that, you know, organ donation is important, but this is how many organ transplants occur in the United States in a year"—about 28,000—"and this is how many abortions"—about 1.2 million. Don't you think if we are talking about organ donations, she had asked the chair, we should talk about abortions, too?

A study published in 2009 by Dr. Steinauer and others found that a third of medical schools include no discussion of elective abortion in the first and second, or preclinical, years. "People don't know what aspect of medicine they're going into" in the preclinical years, she said. If their courses skirt one of the most common procedures, how can they decide?

And in the third year, when students make rounds with physicians, get hands-on training, and decide what kind of doctors they want to be, only a third of them get lectures on abortion, said Douglas W. Laube, a professor at the University of Wisconsin School of Medicine and a former president of the American College of Obstetricians and Gynecologists. "Slightly less than half are offered some sort of a clinical experience," said Dr. Laube, who is also board chair of Physicians for Reproductive Health.

73

By contrast, 84 percent of medical schools cover the mechanism and/or history of Viagra, Dr. Steinauer's study found.

FISCAL PRESSURES

The teaching of abortion is, of course, fraught with controversy. Many medical schools, with active Christian Medical & Dental Associations and other antiabortion groups, are careful about "not offending people," said Michelle Brown, a student at the University of North Carolina's School of Medicine, at the activism meeting.

And state universities rely on legislatures to vote for, and governors to sign, financing measures for new buildings. An administrator, not wanting to offend anti-abortion lawmakers, would be reluctant to "ask why students aren't afforded the opportunity to learn comprehensive reproductive health, including abortion," said Dr. Laube.

Or, as state funds grow scarce, teaching hospitals merge with faith-based ones that object to abortion. In response to such mergers in Seattle, Planned Parenthood expanded its training opportunities to accommodate medical residents.

Access to clinics, where most abortions take place, can be curtailed, as in Toledo. Anti-abortion activists, who once protested at clinics' doors, now lobby for an array of legislative strategies to close them. In North Dakota and elsewhere, new laws, being challenged in the courts, require hospital-admitting privileges for abortion providers, many of whom come from out of state. Given the political climate, hospitals don't want to get involved.

The requirement forced the closure of one of two clinics in Knoxville, Tenn., last year.

COMPLIANCE PROBLEMS

Some medical professionals say preclinical students don't need to learn about abortion. Early medical school "concentrates on anatomy, physiology, and molecular biology, neurobiology," says Dr. Jacobs, of the University of Toledo.

Dr. Jacobs was head of the Medical University of Ohio, which merged with Toledo in 2006, when he was appointed leader of the new institution. He notes that the Accrediting Council for Graduate Medical Education requires abortion training and experience to be offered in ob-gyn residency programs. "Residents at the appropriate level will be exposed to these things," he says.

Indeed, Medical Students for Choice counts the council's requirement among its early successes. Partly a result of the activist group's first nationwide petition drive, the requirement has been in place since 1996. In response, Congress voted to maintain the federal funds and legal status of medical colleges that do not offer abortion training, whether accredited or not.

About 20 percent of the 100 programs reviewed each year are found to be noncompliant, according to the council. They have at least four years to change their curricula before being revisited by the review committee.

While most ob-gyn residencies now offer the training in some form, about 40 percent still don't integrate it into their rotations.

At Toledo, Dr. Jacobs promises to "meet the requirements for all procedures that are required for good practice by the accrediting body," by sending residents to train in other towns "in the immediate vicinity."

But the nearest abortion clinic is in Ann Arbor, Mich., an hour away, says Ms. Payne. Training in another state poses problems with regulations and licensing. And the now-closed Center for Choice trained not only University of Toledo residents but those from Wright State University, in Dayton. Fewer clinics for the same number of residents means more travel and scheduling issues.

Medical Students for Choice lists on its Web site those residencies that offer comprehensive training. The Kenneth J. Ryan program, for example, finances more than 60 such programs at the 242 ob-gyn residencies in the United States. But not only obstetricians provide abortions. Family doctors, surgeons, and other physicians do, too. The accrediting council requires the training only in ob-gyn residencies.

So future residents who want to learn abortion care have to think carefully about where to apply.

Lois Backus, executive director of Medical Students for Choice, came to the group after opening clinics for Planned Parenthood in three states. The biggest challenge, she told the students here, was "finding a doctor." That's not surprising; according to a 2011 study by the Guttmacher Institute, 87 percent of counties in the United States have no abortion providers. And while 97 percent of ob-gyn doctors encountered patients seeking abortions, only 14.4 percent performed them, according to a 2011 study by Debra B. Stulberg, a University of Chicago researcher, and others.

"What will you say," Ms. Backus asked the students in Atlanta, when a member of your family asks, "Why do you have to provide abortions?"

"Sarah," a student from Florida who asked not to use her real name, will soon start her residency in obstetrics. "Because if I don't do them," she replied, "who will?"

This month in Ohio, the Senate added language to a proposed state budget that would forbid public hospitals to make transfer agreements with abortion clinics. If that measure survives, the state would be in the unusual position of requiring the agreements with hospitals while forbidding public hospitals from making them.

"It's a paradox," wrote Ms. Payne, the chapter president, who was back in Ohio, studying for exams. Once those were done, she wrote, she planned to "regroup activism from the med-student end."

1. Do transfer laws serve any purpose other than limiting access to abortion?
2. Do you think preclinical medical students should have the opportunity to learn about abortion procedures? Should this be required? Why or why not?

"TIM KAINE'S ABORTION DISTORTIONS," BY TREVOR THOMAS, FROM *AMERICAN THINKER*, OCTOBER 9, 2016

It takes an immense amount of liberal-speak -- double-talk, gibberish, propaganda, and outright lies -- to attempt to justify the slaughter of children in the womb. Tuesday night, in his debate against Mike Pence, Tim Kaine, the Democrats' nominee for vice president, gave it his best effort.

During the debate, Kaine, a Catholic, reiterated his absurd and long-held position of, "I'm personally opposed to abortion, but I support a woman's right to choose." In order to make people feel okay about voting for a candidate who won't stand up for the defenseless, for decades now Democrats running for office have used the "personally opposed" argument when it comes to abortion.

Renowned Christian thinker Robert P. George, the McCormick Professor of Jurisprudence at Princeton University, satirically (and brilliantly) indicts the "personally opposed" position:

> I am personally opposed to killing abortionists. However, inasmuch as my personal opposition to this practice is rooted in a sectarian (Catholic) religious belief in the sanctity of human life, I am unwilling to impose it on others who may, as a matter of conscience, take a different view. Of course, I am entirely in favor of policies aimed at removing the root causes of violence against abortionists. Indeed, I would go so far as to support mandatory one-week waiting periods, and even nonjudgmental counseling, for people who are contemplating the choice of killing an abortionist. I believe in policies that reduce the urgent need some people feel to kill abortionists while, at the same time, respecting the rights of conscience of my fellow citizens who believe that the killing of abortionists is sometimes a tragic necessity -- not a good, but a lesser evil. In short, I am moderately pro-choice.

Do you suppose Senator Kaine "personally opposes" slavery? I wonder if his car is adorned with the bumper sticker, "Don't like slavery? Then don't own a slave." According to Mr. Kaine's logic, Jeffrey Dahmer's cannibalism was just a "dietary choice;" Hitler and Stalin's genocide was merely a "demographics choice;" and as they execute apostates, members of ISIS are only exercising their "right" to religious liberty.

As *National Review's* Kevin Williamson points out, Tim Kaine's abortion argument (like countless others before him, and no-doubt -- until we all stand face-to-face with the Eternal Truth -- countless more after him) "is incoherent and indefensible; it is, in fact, illiterate." The word "incoherent" came to my mind when Senator Kaine declared, "That's what we ought to be doing in public life: living our lives of faith or motivation with enthusiasm and excitement, convincing each other, dialoguing with each other about important moral issues of the day. But on fundamental issues of morality, we should let women make their own decisions."

When it comes to the morality of life, we as a society often stop people from "making their own decisions." What's more, we often "discriminate" when we do so. For over a year now, my family has wished that someone would have stopped the drug-impaired man who, "making his own decision," got behind the wheel of his truck and struck and killed my beloved father-in-law.

Senator Kaine also declared, "We really feel like you should live fully and with enthusiasm in the commands of your faith, but it is not the role of the public servant to mandate that for everybody else." Kaine seems perilously close to another "incoherent and indefensible" argument: the old tried and untrue, "We shouldn't legislate morality!" As I've noted more than once, all law is rooted in someone's idea of morality. And as I put it in 2013, "It is absurd and ignorant to lament conservative Christian efforts when it comes to abortion, marriage, and so on as some attempt to 'legislate morality.' The other side is attempting the very same thing!"

Mr. Kaine seems stunningly blind to the fact that, whether through the courts or through legislation, the left has long been "mandating for everyone else." Whether abortion, homosexuality, a perverse redefinition of marriage, transgenderism, and so on, for decades the "public servants" on the American left have used the power of the U.S. legal system -- with the threat of fines, jail, and other similar punishments -- to enact and enforce, in other words, to "mandate," the (im)moral agenda of modern liberalism.

Bakers, florists, photographers, wedding hosts, conservative U.S. states, and the like have suffered under our legal system due to their Christian views on marriage and homosexuality. In addition, those corrupted by liberalism in the corporate and entertainment industries (especially the sports entertainment industry) have joined their perverse pals in legislatures and the courts in punishing those who hold to what the Bible reveals on marriage, sex, gender, the family, and so on. So much for allowing those with whom we disagree to "live fully and with enthusiasm in the commands of [their] faith."

Mr. Kaine seems to have no problem allowing his faith to inform his decision-making as a professional when it comes to the death penalty. As the *Daily Beast* recently pointed out,

> Over the course of his career, Kaine didn't just oppose the death penalty; he worked to prevent executions by representing men facing death because they

committed murders ... Since his first days as a lawyer, Kaine has put in hundreds of hours, for free, to get murderers off death row. His first, formative case was [Richard Lee] Whitley's, who confessed to slashing the throat of a 63-year-old woman living in his Fairfax County neighborhood and then using two umbrellas to sexually assault her.

At first, Kaine said no to defending Whitley, but then his selective hypocrite radar went off.

"But then it kind of worked on me that I had said no because my feeling is, well, I say I'm against the death penalty," Kaine told the *Virginian-Pilot* for a 2005 profile. "If I say that's my belief but I say, 'Nah, I'm not going to do it,' then I'm a hypocrite."

Kaine ended up putting in about 1,000 hours for Whitley, who would eventually -- and justly -- be executed. After Whitley's just sentence was carried out, Kaine declared, "Murder is wrong in the gulag, in Afghanistan, in Soweto, in the mountains of Guatemala, in Fairfax County ... and even the Spring Street Penitentiary." Liberal logic at its finest: executing a throat-slashing rapist is "murder," but killing the most innocent and defenseless among us is a "choice."

"And he cited his faith," the *Daily Beast* adds, then quotes Kaine concluding: "I think it's outrageous that there is the death penalty. It's not the biggest outrage in the world, but it's one of a number of outrageous [things] where people don't appropriately value the sanctity of human life." Again, according to Kaine's twisted logic we should "value" the life of murderers (who themselves have shown a callous disregard for human life), but not the unborn. Amazing.

And notice what's absent from Kaine's personal "pro-life" activism? For a man who's "personally opposed" to abortion, other than not having an abortion himself (If liberals think men can have babies, can't they also have an abortion?), Mr. Kaine seems to have done almost nothing to help the plight of the unborn. In his mind, he's a "hypocrite" for not standing up for murderers, but that doesn't apply when it comes to the unborn. Again, amazing. Sadly, it seems Kaine has done a wonderful job of humanizing the worst among us and dehumanizing the least among us.

Lastly, Kaine's notion that, if Donald Trump has his way, women who have abortions will face legal consequences ignores the fact that, when abortion was illegal across the U.S., the law targeted abortionists, not pregnant women. State laws treated women as the second "victim" of abortion.

As Williamson concludes, when it comes to abortion, Tim Kaine is an intellectual mess and a moral coward, and as Matt Walsh puts it, a heretic as well. In other words, he's the perfect candidate to run alongside Hillary Clinton.

1. Is it contradictory to oppose abortion personally but support a woman's right to choose, as Tim Kaine does?

2. Do you agree with the author's statement that "[b]akers, florists, photographers, wedding hosts, conservative U.S. states, and the like have suffered under our legal system due to their Christian views on marriage and homosexuality"?

CHAPTER 3

WHAT THE COURTS SAY

Legal restrictions against abortion have been a mainstay throughout American history. Purportedly, these laws existed to protect would-be mothers from unsafe procedures. Arguably however, judges and lawmakers (generally men) wished to exercise disproportionate influence over the reproductive process. By 1965, not one of the fifty states allowed legal abortions, although some exceptions applied, as in cases when the life of the mother was endangered, or the mother was a victim of rape or incest.

The Supreme Court ushered in an entirely new paradigm with the historical 1973 ruling in *Roe v. Wade*. For the first time in the nation's history, most state restrictions against abortion were deemed unconstitutional. According to the court's seven to two decision, states could not impose any barriers to abortion within the first trimester of a pregnancy. Between weeks thirteen and twenty-eight, the states were allowed to "reasonably" regulate abortion as they saw fit. In the third trimester, abortions are completely forbidden, unless it is required to save the life or preserve the health of the mother.

As we saw in the previous chapter, states have proposed novel ways to restrict abortion rights, imposing onerous demands on the physical facilities of clinics, waiting periods, and other ploys to inconvenience or otherwise dissuade a woman seeking an abortion. In response to Texas House Bill 2 (HB 2), the organization Whole Woman's Health filed a recent lawsuit claiming that these laws placed "undue burdens" on women seeking abortions. The court ruled in favor of the plaintiffs, striking down HB 2 as unconstitutional.

The high court has also reviewed another set of cases involving challenges to the Affordable Care Act's provision for contraceptives under existing health care plans, which has itself been targeted by President Donald Trump. Some corporations and religious groups have claimed that providing contraceptives to employees violates their religious freedom. One problem with this claim is that companies can opt out of providing contraceptive coverage, simply by filing a form. Once complete, this form exempts the organization from any involvement, turning the costs of contraceptives over to the government. While the court has been sympathetic to some corporate claims of religious freedom, most notably that of the chain Hobby Lobby, it remains to be seen how far reaching the religious exemption will be in limiting contraceptive coverage.

Although there are few signs that *Roe* will be overturned outright, abortion advocates have been forced to play defense in the courts, as new challenges to reproductive freedom continue to be heard with distressing regularity.

"BARRIER METHOD? U.S. SUPREME COURT TO HEAR NEW GROUP OF CASES THAT COULD FURTHER LIMIT AMERICANS' ACCESS TO REPRODUCTIVE HEALTH CARE," BY SIMON BROWN, FROM *CHURCH AND STATE*, JANUARY 2016

Political allies of the Religious Right, like U.S. Sen. Ted Cruz (R-Texas), are trying to convince the American public that the federal government wants to force nuns to buy birth control.

"You know, every American should know about the Little Sisters of the Poor," Cruz said during an address at the Family Research Council's Values Voter Summit in Washington, D.C., in 2014. "You want to talk about values? Right now the federal government is suing the Little Sisters of the Poor to try to force Catholic nuns to pay for abortion-inducing drugs. "

Cruz's comments came in reference to legal challenges filed by dozens of religiously affiliated non-profit organizations, including the Little Sisters of the Poor, that don't want their employees to get access to birth control.

The groups are dissatisfied with an accommodation that already exempts them from an Affordable Care Act [ACA) requirement that most employers must provide their employees with insurance plans that cover contraceptives. Despite that exemption, the nuns, who run a chain of homes for the elderly, sued the federal government – not the other way around – because they believe their "religious freedom" is at risk when their employees, many of whom likely don't share the nuns' views on birth control, have access to certain forms of medical care.

To Cruz, a Tea Party hero and GOP presidential hopeful, these nuns are emblematic of the Obama administration's supposed war against religion.

The reality, however, is very different. Both for-profit corporations and religiously affiliated non-profits that object to offering employee healthcare plans that include birth control must simply sign a two-page form stating their objection to the ACA's so-called contraceptive mandate. They also have the option of sending the government a letter stating their objection and providing some basic information.

Once the form or letter is submitted, the government takes care of the rest to make contraceptives available to employees who want them. The employer is in no way obligated to endorse birth control, let alone pay for it. But even that basic form or letter is too much for some organizations, which claim that their "religious freedom" is somehow burdened if their employees use birth control – regardless of who pays for it.

If this complaint by a group of Catholic nuns sounds extreme to you, then you are of the same mind as most federal courts. Seven out of eight U.S. appellate courts to have considered this matter have rejected the argument that the act of opting out of the ACA is a burden to religious belief. But when a panel of the 8th U.S. Circuit Court of Appeals sided with a few of these non-profits in September, it virtually assured that the U.S. Supreme Court would take up the issue.

Indeed, on Nov. 6 the high court announced it will hear seven consolidated cases in yet another challenge to a provision of the ACA. Although the cases before the high court this time involve non-profit organizations, the challenged accommodation was also made available to for-profit corporations following the 2014 decision in *Burwell v. Hobby Lobby Stores*. So if the non-profit employers in these cases win, observers expect for-profit corporations such as Hobby Lobby to challenge the accommodation too, once again putting the health-care needs of tens of thousands of employees at risk.

Of the seven consolidated cases, the best known is *Little Sisters of the Poor Home for the Aged v. Burwell*. The Colorado-based Little Sisters have waged an effective public-relations war throughout their legal challenge to the ACA, making sure to put a group of nuns front and center whenever they address the media about their case.

This is deliberate. It leads casual observers to wonder why the Obama administration would expect a bunch of devout Catholics to buy birth control.

The people you don't see at press conferences are the men and women who are employed by the plaintiffs in these cases — many of whom likely rely on safe and effective birth control.

The nuns claim that signing a form or writing a short letter to protect these employees "would make them morally complicit in grave sin" because it somehow "triggers" the use of abortion-inducing drugs. (The contraceptives in question, medical experts agree, don't cause abortions.)

The abortion issue is a smokescreen. The nuns seek to block their employees from using any form of birth control—even the ubiquitous birth control pill, which the vast majority of American women use at some point in their lives.

"On the ... mandate issue, the government basically forced us into a corner," Sister Constance Carolyn of the Little Sisters wrote in an email last March to the *Atlantic*. "We have no desire to litigate against our government, but we had no choice because we cannot participate in the moral evil of providing or facilitating the provision of abortion and contraception. So the government has put us in a very real bind."

This public-relations campaign has earned the Little Sisters some powerful friends. Besides Cruz, former Arkansas Gov. Mike Huckabee, another GOP presidential hopeful, defended the nuns in September – while also attacking President Barack Obama.

"Here's a person who says he's a Christian, all right let's take it at face value, let's just say that's correct," Huckabee said of Obama during an interview with Fox News' Sean Hannity. "But what kind of Christian? What kind of Christian goes after the Little Sisters of the Poor?"

Huckabee and other right-wingers who have commented on the case consistently fail to mention the numerous people in the employ of the Little Sisters who not only aren't nuns but who may not even agree with Catholic doctrine on the use of birth control. (The nuns' view is so strict most U.S. Catholics reject it.)

For example, the Little Sisters website notes that its Denver facility has "a staff of professional men and women and over 60 volunteers."

The Little Sisters run homes for the aged all over the country, and they employ many people as care-takers, food-service workers and maintenance staff. These modest-wage jobs are often filled by women – and many of them want and expect access to birth control in their health-care plan.

While they've been successful in manipulating public opinion, the nuns have fared less well in court. In July, the U.S. 10th Circuit Court of Appeals was not sympathetic to the nuns' argument, ruling that the act of opting out of the ACA contraceptive coverage regulations does not infringe on the religious-liberty rights of the Little Sisters under the Religious Freedom Restoration Act (RFRA), a 1993 federal law designed to protect religious liberty.

"[T]he accommodation relieves Plaintiffs of their obligation to provide, pay for, or facilitate contraceptive coverage, and does so without substantially burdening their religious exercise," the decision read.

The Becket Fund for Religious Liberty, a Washington, D.C.-based conservative legal group that represents the Little Sisters, did not see it that way; the group began hyperbolically asserting that the federal government wants to turn Catholic organizations into birth control dispensaries.

"The government keeps digging the hole deeper," said Adele Auxier Keim, Becket Fund legal counsel, in a July 10 statement. "[T]he government still won't give up on its quest to force nuns and other religious employers to distribute contraceptives."

But not even the 5th U.S. Circuit Court of Appeals, which is presided over by some of the most conservative judges in the nation, bought into the idea that filling out a form is a religious burden. In another non-profit case, *East Texas Baptist University v. Burwell*, Judge Jerry E. Smith – an appointee of President Ronald W. Reagan – wrote that the school is not required to provide contraceptives or do anything else that would violate its religious beliefs.

"The payments for contraceptives are completely independent of the plans ..., " Smith wrote. "The acts that violate their faith are the acts of the government, insurers, and third-party administrators, but R.F.R.A. does not entitle them to block third parties from engaging in conduct with which they disagree."

As in *Hobby Lobby*, these cases turn on the inter-pretation of RFRA. But there are important differences. In *Hobby Lobby,* the Supreme Court had to consider whether requiring a for-profit corporation whose owners had a reli-gious objection to paying directly for birth control coverage violates RFRA. This time, the high court must decide whether the mere act of filling out a form or writing a letter to opt out of certain health-care coverage places a substantial burden on the beliefs of religiously affiliated non-profits.

Observers have already begun to speculate how the Supreme Court will decide in this matter, using *Hobby Lobby* as a guide. In that 2014 decision, Justice Samuel A. Alito wrote that the Obama administration's accommodation for religious groups like the Little Sisters "does not impinge on the plaintiffs' religious beliefs." He also suggested that the government could extend this accommodation to for-profit groups like *Hobby Lobby,* which is exactly what happened in July of last year.

Justice Anthony M. Kennedy, who is generally viewed as the swing vote in contentious cases like *Hobby Lobby* and will perhaps be the tie breaker in the non-profit contraception decision, hinted in his concurring *Hobby Lobby* opinion that he would not strike down the Obama administration's accommodation for non-profits.

"The accommodation works by requiring insurance companies to cover, without cost sharing, contraception coverage for female employees who wish it," Kennedy wrote. "That accommodation equally furthers the Government's interest but does not impinge on the plaintiff's religious beliefs."

Kevin Martin, a former law clerk for Justice Antonin Scalia, told *The Huffington Post* that Kennedy's words in particular should trouble the Little Sisters and their allies. Kennedy "goes out of his way in the other direction to say the accommodation does not burden religious exercise rights," Martin said. "It may be that because he didn't have the Little Sisters case before him, you can't read too much into it, but it should give the plaintiffs cause for concern. "

Americans United will weigh in on this issue with an amicus brief in the coming months. AU previously filed a brief in the Little Sisters case in which it argued that absolutely no harm is being done to non-profits that are required to do nothing beyond state their objection to contraceptives.

"A burden is not substantial under RFRA simply because a litigant says so ...," the brief asserted.

Americans United Senior Litigation Counsel Gregory M. Lipper, who will work on AU's upcoming brief, said previously that no further accommodation is needed to protect the rights of religiously affiliated non-profits.

"These cases are not about whether employers have to provide coverage for birth control: The government has already exempted them from doing so," said Lipper in a November statement. "But the plaintiffs refuse to take yes for answer. Instead, they claim the right to prevent their employees from getting contraceptive coverage from third parties, who will be providing the coverage and no cost to – and with no involvement from – the plaintiffs. "

Of course, the high court could set all of those previous considerations aside and adopt the view of the only federal appeals court that sided with a religious non-profit challenging the ACA accommodation. In its decisions in *Sharpe Holdings, Inc. v. U.S. Department of Health and Human Services* and *Dordt College v. Burwell,* which were issued in September, a panel of the 8th U.S. Circuit Court of Appeals said an organization's belief that opting out of the ACA mandate "triggers" abortions is sufficient.

"[W]e conclude that by coercing Dordt and Cornerstone to participate in the contraceptive mandate and accommodation process under threat of severe monetary penalty, the government has substantially burdened Dordt and Cornerstone's exercise of religion" and "that, even assuming that the government's interests in safeguarding public health and ensuring equal access to health care for women are compelling, the contraceptive mandate and accommodation process likely are not the least restrictive means of furthering those interests," wrote Judge Roger Wollman.

Americans United, which filed an amicus brief in these cases along with its allies, strongly disagreed with the 8th Circuit's position.

"The employers in these cases are giving the noble concept of religious freedom a bad name," said Barry W. Lynn, executive director of Americans United, in a press statement. "They want to use the Religious Freedom Restoration Act to gain tremendous power for themselves at the expense of untold numbers of women. That is not how it should work in this country, and I sincerely hope the Supreme Court agrees."

If the high court does not agree, however, the consequences could be dire.

"While the plaintiffs in these cases are all non-profit organizations, if they succeed then employees of for-profit corporations – including multibillion dollar chains like Hobby Lobby – will also be left in the lurch," Lipper said. "In fact, in ruling for Hobby Lobby last year, the Supreme Court told the government to extend this accommodation to for-profit companies, so that those companies' employees could receive contraceptive coverage from third parties. If even the accommodation is struck down, tens of thousands of employees who work for for-profit corporations will lose contraceptive coverage as well. "

It's an alarming scenario, and by late June the nation will know whether or not it has come to pass.

1. How are non-profit organizations that oppose the use of contraceptives arguing that the Affordable Care Act's "opt-out" provision violates their religious freedom? Is there any merit to their position?

2. How do you balance a private company's religious beliefs with the needs of their employees? If a company like Hobby Lobby refuses to pay for contraceptives, would forcing them to infringe on their religious freedom?

"BEHIND THE SUPREME COURT'S ABORTION DECISION, MORE THAN A DECADE OF PRIVATELY FUNDED RESEARCH," BY NINA MARTIN, FROM *PROPUBLICA*, JULY 14, 2016

THIS STORY WAS CO-PUBLISHED WITH MOTHER JONES.

Back in January, as the Supreme Court was preparing for its most important abortion case in a generation, some four dozen social scientists submitted a brief explaining why they believed key portions of Texas law HB2 should be struck down. The brief was a 58-page compendium of research on everything from the relative dangers of abortion vs. childbirth to the correlation between abortion barriers and postpartum depression. "In this politically charged area, it is particularly important that assertions about health and safety are evaluated using reliable scientific evidence," the researchers declared.

Six months later, the material they submitted clearly helped shape Justice Stephen Breyer's majority opinion in *Whole Woman's Health v. Hellerstedt*, which found critical elements of HB2 unconstitutional. Less noticed, the decision also handed a resounding victory to private donors who've spent more than a decade quietly pouring at least $200 million into the scientists' work, creating an influential abortion-research complex that has left abortion opponents in the dust.

The research initiative dates back at least to the early 2000s and became more urgent after the high court suggested in 2007 that in cases of "medical and scientific uncertainty," legislatures could have "wide discretion" to pass laws restricting abortion. Since then, a primary objective of abortion rights supporters has been to establish a high level of medical certainty — both about the safety of the procedure and about what happens when a woman's reproductive options are drastically curtailed or eliminated.

There's little or no publicly funded research on this controversial topic in the U.S., so for years basic information was lacking — from how often patients have complications to what happens to women who want abortions but can't obtain them.

Into this breach stepped the Susan Thompson Buffett Foundation, named for the late wife of one of the richest men in the world. Established in the 1960s, the philanthropic behemoth (it ranked fourth among family foundations in 2014 in terms of giving) is known for its focus on abortion access, training and more recently, prevention. It's also known for its secrecy, often appearing under grant acknowledgements only as "an anonymous donor."

The Buffett Foundation helped finance the development of the abortion drug RU–486 back in the 1990s. From 2001 to 2014, it contributed more than $1.5 billion to abortion causes, including at least $427 million to Planned Parenthood worldwide and $168 million to the National Abortion Federation — a track record that led one foe to call Warren Buffett the "sugar daddy of the entire pro-abortion movement." In the past 15 years, it has also made research a core part of its strategic efforts, funding such organizations as the Guttmacher Institute, a policy think tank and advocacy group that tracks demographic and legislative trends ($40 million), and Gynuity Health Projects, which focuses on medication abortion ($29 million), as well as work by academics abroad. Other foundations supporting research on a smaller scale have included the William and Flora Hewlett Foundation, the David and Lucile Packard Foundation, the John Merck Fund, and the Educational Foundation of America. (Hewlett is also a funder of ProPublica.)

Buffett's main academic partner (receiving at least $88 million from 2001 to 2014) has been the University of California, San Francisco, a medical research institution with a strong reproductive-health infrastructure. (Abortion opponents' perspective is a bit different: "America's abortion training academy," one National Right to Life official recently called it). Historically, "it's very unusual for foundations to fund research," Tracy Weitz, former director of UCSF's Advancing New Standards in Reproductive Health project (ANSIRH, pronounced "answer"), told ProPublica in 2013. But in the last 10 or 12 years, "there's been recognition in the philanthropic community that in order to make progress, either culturally or politically or in the service-delivery arena, there are research questions that we need to answer."

Located in the state with the most liberal record on reproductive rights, UCSF has been able to do pioneering studies without the kind of political interference that might be expected elsewhere. Indeed, California lawmakers have granted special protections for people who work in the reproductive health field, while state health agencies worked to facilitate a potentially controversial project that involved training non-doctors to perform abortions. The ANSIRH program was established in 2002 as part of UCSF's Bixby Center for Global Reproductive Health and lists more than two dozen separate abortion-related initiatives on its website on everything from mandatory ultrasound-viewing laws to abortion in movies and TV to reproductive health access for women in the military. Funder and fundee have been closely intertwined; Weitz left UCSF to become the Buffett Foundation's director of U.S. programs in 2014.

Well before the Texas case, foundation-backed researchers had already begun to churn out studies aimed at debunking some of the most common justifications for new abortion restrictions: that clinics were teeming with incompetent doctors; that injured, abandoned patients were flooding emergency rooms; that the psychological damage caused by grief and regret after abortions often persists for years and ruins women's lives.

In the past three years, their findings have influenced a string of policy changes —prompting the Food and Drug Administration to revise its labeling guidelines for abortion drugs, persuading the Iowa Supreme Court to uphold a telemedicine program for medication abortion, and convincing the California legislature to allow health care professionals besides doctors to perform first-trimester abortions.

The proliferation of so-called Targeted Regulation of Abortion Provider, or TRAP, laws like HB2 — which purport to protect women's safety and health by imposing tough rules on clinics and doctors — provided the research effort with its greatest test, yet also an opportunity to put its findings to potent effect.

Buffett Foundation money underwrote the Texas Policy Evaluation Project, a small band of demographers, doctors, and public health specialists based at the University of Texas at Austin who came together in 2011, when lawmakers slashed family-planning funding, kicked Planned Parenthood out of the Medicaid women's health program, and required sonograms 24 hours before abortions. "We realized that this was going to have devastating impact on the reproductive health and safety network in the state," said Daniel Grossman, an investigator for the project who also teaches at UCSF and replaced Weitz as ANSIRH's director last year.

Then, in 2013, the legislature passed HB2, an omnibus bill that required abortion clinics to upgrade their facilities to surgical-center standards, mandated doctors to have admitting privileges at local hospitals, imposed new restrictions on medication abortion, and banned abortion after 20 weeks. The TRAP provisions shuttered almost half of the state's 41 clinics practically overnight, with stark consequences, the project found. The abortion rate dropped by 13 percent and medication abortions by 70 percent. Travel distances and costs soared and wait times sometimes stretched for weeks, leading to a 27 percent increase in more dangerous (and more expensive) second-trimester procedures. Some women considered self-inducing. Some unhappily carried their pregnancies to term. Meanwhile, part of HB2 was on hold pending the Supreme Court ruling; if it went into effect, another eight to 10 clinics would shut and the few clinics that remained would be inundated. "They didn't really seem to have the capacity to increase their services," Grossman said. "It was really concerning."

The 5-to–3 majority ruling in *Hellerstedt* read like a recitation of the researchers' findings, declaring the Texas laws served no real medical purpose and created an undue burden on women's constitutional rights. Within days, TRAP laws also toppled in Mississippi, Wisconsin and Alabama, and abortion rights groups announced plans to challenge other types of laws — for example, 72-hour waiting periods and bans on abortions after 20 weeks. "Abortion restrictions cannot rely on junk science," said Stephanie Toti, an attorney with the Center for Reproductive Rights (more than $20 million in Buffett funding since 2001). "There has to be credible scientific evidence to support the law, and there has to be a determination that the benefits of the law outweigh the harm."

Some abortion opponents have been quick to argue that the research is not credible, in some cases because the people who do it are biased. Justice Samuel Alito insisted the Texas Policy Evaluation Project's analysis of clinic closures and capacity was unconvincing. "Research is fine when it illuminates an issue," Randall O'Bannon, education and research director for National Right to Life, told a reporter for his organization's news site. But the findings were "crafted to protect the interests of the abortion industry with scant attention to the legitimate health and safety issues of Texas women, let alone unborn babies."

The anti-abortion movement has recently attempted to launch its own research initiative. The Charlotte Lozier Institute was established in 2011 as a policy think tank alternative to Guttmacher. The American Association of Pro-Life Obstetricians and Gynecologists holds annual conferences at which researchers who oppose abortion discuss studies they've done on links between abortion and breast cancer, depression and drug abuse and hold workshops on how to serve as expert witnesses. But those operations are minuscule compared to those of Buffett and ANSIRH. "The pro-choice research seems to have almost unlimited funds," Bowling Green State University's Priscilla Coleman lamented at this winter's AAPLOG meeting. So far, researchers funded by abortion opponents lack the infrastructure to conduct the kind of data collection and analysis that academic institutions have done. "Picking the right groups to compare, following them for a long period of time, so that you can really see what the outcomes are — it's long and it's hard and it's costly," UCSF's Rana Barar said.

Abortion opponents have often seen data and scientific evidence as almost beside the point, acknowledged Lozier's president, Chuck Donovan. "For most people on the pro-life side of the debate, abortion is primarily an ethical, moral, for some a religious challenge." As a result, "a statistical base, an analytical base has gone a little bit undernourished." Individual researchers have been stymied by mainstream medical hostility, Steven Aden, senior counsel at the conservative legal powerhouse Alliance Defending Freedom, said this spring. "It is extraordinarily difficult to get even a solid study peer-reviewed and published," he said. And when it does happen, "because the politics are against them they are subjected to a beat-down campaign, sometimes even when what they're arguing is fairly straightforward." Often the best those efforts could hope to achieve was to "generate uncertainty," as Mary Ziegler, a law professor at Florida State University and author of "After Roe: The Lost History of the Abortion Debate," put it. Before *Hellerstedt*, that was often seen as enough: "The idea was if there's uncertainty, the tie-breaker goes to the lawmakers," Ziegler said.

Even before the Texas decision, abortion foes had begun to shift away from women's health and safety, instead expanding on existing restrictions (such as longer mandatory waiting periods and tougher parental consent laws) and renewing the focus on protecting fetuses: "The science of fetal development is a burgeoning area," Aden said.

Researchers funded by the Buffett Foundation and others, meanwhile, have mounted projects that look at the impact of abortion restrictions in Georgia, Utah, Ohio and Tennessee.

"The role of research and the nature of relevant research will be different in different contexts," CRR's Toti said. "But what the court made clear is that abortion restrictions are going to be evaluated on an evidence-based standard. States can no longer rely on speculation about the potential benefits of a law." The question now, she said, is "what actual benefit does a regulation provide and how does that compare with the extent of the burden a law is going to impose on women."

1. Are there any potential drawbacks to a privately-funded reproductive rights movement?

2. Now that scientific research has invalidated the purported motives of many so-called TRAP laws, how do you predict abortion opponents might respond?

"THE ROE OF MARRIAGE: TRADITIONALISTS SHOULD DEFEND THEIR CONCEPTION OF THE TRUTH," BY RYAN T. ANDERSON, FROM THE *NATIONAL REVIEW*, AUG 11 2014

Before *Roe v. Wade* in 1973, no one could have predicted that the Supreme Court would effectively create a national regime of abortion on demand throughout all nine months of pregnancy. The ruling was simply more sweeping and more extreme than anyone had expected.

But what if we had a crystal ball and a time machine and could travel back to 1972? What would we do if we could see *Roe* looming on the horizon? What would we do to prevent such a disastrous ruling? What would we do to minimize the harm that it would cause? And what plans would we put in place to make our response to *Roe*, if it were handed down anyway, more constructive?

This is the situation that supporters of marriage face today. Since the Supreme Court decision last June on the federal Defense of Marriage Act (DOMA), a string of lower courts have struck down state marriage laws, setting up a return of the issue to the high court. Public-opinion polling (especially of my peers in the Millennial generation), the forced resignation of Mozilla founder Brendan Eich, and the defeat of Arizona's religious-liberty bill all make the situation seem dire.

And our progressive elites would like the millions of Americans who continue to believe that marriage is what societies have always believed it to be—a male-female union—to get with the program and accept the inevitable. Clearly, they tell us, we're on the Wrong Side of History.

But we should avoid the temptation to prognosticate about the future in lieu of working to shape that future. We are citizens in a self-governing society, not pundits watching a spectator sport, not subjects of rulers. We are participants in one of the most significant debates any society has ever had.

And we must do whatever we can in service of the ultimate goal of restoring a culture of marriage. In the short run, the legal battle may be an uphill struggle. But in the long run, those who defend marriage as the union of a man and a woman will prove to have been prophetic. After all, the logic of marriage redefinition ultimately leads to the dissolution of marriage, to a social mess of adult love of manifold sizes and shapes. Defenders of the truth about marriage should redouble our efforts while there is still time to steer clear of that chaos.

Like pro-lifers, we should start by building alliances with those concerned about judicial activism and committed to sound federalism. In the run-up to *Roe*, the rallying cry should have been that the Constitution is silent on the question of abortion—and so the people remain sovereign. Now we must defend our constitutional authority as citizens to make marriage policy.

As Judge Paul Kelly of the Tenth Circuit recently explained, we do not need a single, 50-state answer from the courts: "If the States are the laboratories of democracy, requiring every state to recognize same-gender unions—contrary to the views of its electorate and representatives—turns the notion of a limited national government on its head."

Indeed, last summer, when the Supreme Court struck down DOMA, Chief Justice John Roberts emphasized in his dissent the limits of the majority's opinion. He clarified that neither the holding nor its logic required redefining state marriage laws.

Justice Scalia predicted in his dissent that the Court would do whatever it thought it could get away with. We must therefore make clear that court-imposed same-sex marriage via a *Roe*-style decision will not settle the marriage debate any more than it has settled the abortion debate.

Whatever the Court does will cause less damage if we vigorously defend a classically liberal form of limited government and highlight the importance of religious liberty. Even if the Court were to redefine marriage, government should not require third parties to recognize a same-sex relationship as a marriage. After all, protecting religious liberty and the rights of conscience does not infringe on anyone's sexual freedom.

Yet in a growing number of incidents, the redefinition of marriage and state policies on sexual orientation have burdened the freedoms of citizens who believe that marriage is the union of a man and a woman. Florists, photographers, family bakeries, and adoption agencies, among others, have faced penalties and lawsuits or been driven out of business for working in accordance with their convictions.

Ultimately, we cannot protect religious liberty without defending our substantive views. This is one key lesson from the pro-life movement. While liberal elites disagree with the pro-life position, many at least understand why a pro-life citizen holds the views she does, and why government thus shouldn't coerce citizens into performing or subsidizing abortions. Will those who favor marriage redefinition view—and thus treat—their dissenting fellow citizens as, in the words of Justice Scalia, "enemies of the human race"? Or will they treat us as they do pro-lifers?

Just as the pro-life movement explained why its members care about the unborn, we must help our fellow citizens understand why we believe what we do about marriage. Even if they keep their convictions, they might well acknowledge the reasonableness of ours, and respect our right to govern our lives in accord with them.

But too many of our neighbors equate our beliefs with the hate-driven credo of Westboro Baptist's Fred Phelps. If he's the only voice they've heard on marriage, it's hard to blame them.

We must work harder so that they hear our voices. In doing this, we must understand that many of our neighbors haven't rejected the argument for marriage; they simply haven't heard it. We must make that argument in new and creative ways.

Roughly two years ago, Sherif Girgis, Robert P. George, and I published the book *What Is Marriage?* In it we argue that at stake in our national debate are two competing views of what marriage is, and we make a philosophical argument that the conjugal view of marriage is correct.

That view has long informed the law—along with the art, philosophy, religion, and social practice—of our civilization. Marriage, so understood, is a comprehensive union. It unites spouses at all levels of their being: hearts, minds, and bodies, through the two-in-one-flesh union of a man and woman. As the act that unites spouses can also create new life, marriage is especially apt for procreation and family life. Uniting spouses in these all-encompassing ways, marriage calls for all-encompassing commitment: permanent and exclusive.

The state cares about marriage because of its ability to unite children with their mother and father. Marriage increases the odds that a man will be committed both to the children that he helps create and to the woman with whom he does so.

Comprehensive union capable of uniting children with their mom and dad is something only a man and a woman can form. So enacting same-sex marriage would not expand the institution of marriage, but redefine it. Finishing what policies like no-fault divorce began, it would finally replace the conjugal view with a revisionist view of marriage as fundamentally an emotional union. This would multiply the marriage revolution's harms, making them harder than ever to reverse.

Most Americans haven't thought about these dimensions of the debate, but my experience on scores of college campuses during the past year suggests there is hope. After almost every lecture, students approached me to say that they had never heard a rational case for marriage. Christians often said that they always knew marriage was between a man and a woman, but never knew how to defend it as a policy and legal matter.

Students who identified as liberal also admitted that this was the first time they had heard a rational case for marriage. They told me that they respected the argument—and, frequently, that they weren't sure why it was wrong, even if they continued to insist that it was. While we may not be able to convert the most committed, we should seek to soften their resolve to eliminate us from polite society.

And yet naysayers claim that rational arguments never convince. There is something perverse in conservatives' thinking that ideas have consequences but that good ideas can't persuade. Good ideas can persuade, as witnessed by the successes of the pro-life movement—but only if we are willing to present them in a winsome manner. In the long run, the truth wins.

Truth needs a messenger. We must be bolder, better organized, and more strategic, and we must exercise greater foresight when engaging on this issue. We need conservative intellectual forces—think tanks, scholars, religious leaders, and politicians—to actively engage.

Creating such a network is what the pro-life movement has done for 40 years. The free-market movement did something similar: Citizens committed to economic freedom backed their beliefs with their billfolds and built a network of well-funded free-market think tanks and advocacy groups, university programs and scholarship competitions, media groups and marketing campaigns. While social conservatives have made great strides, we still have a ways to go.

No matter what, religious institutions will play a central role in shaping opinions on marriage. Those who choose to remain rather silent will shape opinion by default. But those who rise to the occasion can develop a compelling response to the sexual revolution.

The same was true of the pro-life movement. The Southern Baptists back then, we sometimes forget, were in favor of abortion rights and supported *Roe*. Today they are at the forefront of the cause for life. This should caution us not to write off those who today might be on the wrong side of the marriage debate.

Whatever happens, it is essential to take the long view and to be ready to bear witness to the truth, even if law and culture grow increasingly hostile. There are lessons to be learned from the pro-life movement here too.

Consider February 1973, just weeks after *Roe*. Public opinion ran against it, by a margin of two to one. With each passing day, another pro-life public figure— Ted Kennedy, Jesse Jackson, Al Gore, Bill Clinton— "evolved" to embrace abortion on demand. The media kept insisting that all the young people were for abortion rights. Elites ridiculed pro-lifers as being on the wrong side of history. The pro-lifers were aging; their children, increasingly against them.

But courageous pro-lifers put their hand to the plow, and today we reap the fruits—a majority of Americans are pro-life. Everything the pro-life movement did needs to happen again, but on this new frontier of marriage.

1. Despite its extreme conservatism, do any of the author's views, such as limited federal government and states' rights to experiment with democracy, have any merit, in your opinion?

2. The author draws parallels between *Roe v. Wade* and the Supreme Court's recent decision against the so-called Defense of Marriage Act (DOMA). Does this comparison resonate with you, or is it a false equivalency?

"AT THE COURT: WOMEN'S RIGHTS AT STAKE," BY DIPTI SINGH, FROM *WOMEN'S HEALTH ACTIVIST*, MAY-JUNE 2016

The U.S. Supreme Court is considering two cases that could profoundly impact women's rights and access to essential reproductive health care services. The Supreme Court heard oral arguments in both cases in March. This article gives you an update on those cases; we will also report on the final decisions (expected by July) and next steps.

WHOLE WOMAN'S HEALTH V. HELLERSTEDT

This case challenges a Texas law, House Bill 2 (HB 2),[1] which requires any clinic providing abortion services to meet the same hospital-like building standards required for ambulatory surgical centers. It also requires doctors who provide abortions to have admitting privileges at a hospital within 30 miles from where they perform the procedure.

In the 1992 *Planned Parenthood v. Casey* decision, a divided U.S. Supreme Court reaffirmed *Roe v. Wade's* "core holding," recognizing a woman's constitutionally protected right to choose to have an abortion.[2] The Court held that states can impose restrictions on this right, as long as the restrictions do not impose an "undue burden" on the woman. Under Casey, a state cannot implement a law with either the "purpose or effect" of imposing a "substantial obstacle" to a woman seeking a pre-viability abortion.[3]

Texas claims that HB 2 is needed to protect women's health and safety. The Center for Reproductive Rights (CRR), which is representing the Texas clinics, says the reality is exactly the opposite. It argues that the burdensome requirements are medically unnecessary and fail to promote the safety of abortion care or a woman's health (abortion is, in fact, already one of the safest and most common medical procedures). Instead, the requirements are designed to shut down abortion clinics, and thereby reduce access to legal abortions. Indeed, leading medical experts, including the American Medical Association and the American College of Obstetricians and Gynecologists, submitted an amicus curiae (friend-of-the-court) brief to the Court opposing HB 2. Their brief makes clear that the Texas requirements are contrary to accepted medical practice, unsupported by scientific evidence, and not related to the quality or safety of abortion-related medical care.[4]

If HB 2 goes into effect, fewer than 10 abortion facilities will be able to comply with the onerous regulations in the entire state of Texas. In a state with 5.4 million women of reproductive age, HB 2 would shutter most abortion clinics, forcing many women to travel more than 150 miles to the nearest abortion provider. Even more, if the Court upholds the Texas restrictions, similar (and possibly even more onerous measures) will be introduced and implemented elsewhere in the country. According to the Guttmacher Institute, between

2011 and 2015, 288 abortion-related restrictions were enacted by the state legislatures.[5]

Justice Scalia's recent death is likely to impact the Court's decision. If the four liberal justices (Justices Ginsburg, Breyer, Kagan, and Sotomayor) decide for the clinics (i.e., against the restrictions), and Justice Kennedy joins the conservatives (Chief Justice Roberts and Justices Thomas and Alito) in support of Texas (i.e., upholding the restrictions), the Court will split 4-4. If this happens, the Court has a few options. It could decide to let stand the Fifth's Circuit's decision that CRR is appealing; this decision, which upheld HB 2, would apply to the states in the Fifth Circuit (Texas, Louisiana, and Mississippi). But, the decision would not set national precedent. Alternatively, the Court could decide not to issue a decision at all and, instead, hold the case until the 2016-2017 term or when Congress confirms a ninth justice.

If, instead, Justice Kennedy joins the Court's liberal justices, the Court could issue a 5-3 decision in favor of the clinics and against HB 2. The case would then set nationwide precedent. Its precise impact—in Texas and across the country; for abortion care and in the other contexts--will depend on the breadth or narrowness of the majority's ruling.

ZUBIK V. BURWELL

The other case before the Court is *Zubik v. Burwell*—a consolidation of seven lawsuits by non-profit organizations bringing yet more challenges to the Affordable Care Act (ACA) and the contraceptive coverage requirement.[6] To date, over 100 lawsuits challenging the contraceptive coverage requirement have been filed in Federal courts across the U.S.

The ACA's contraceptive coverage rule requires most new health plans to cover all Food and Drug Administration-approved contraceptive methods, sterilization, and related education and counseling without cost-sharing (no co-pays, deductibles, or co-insurance). Federal regulations exempt houses of worship from the requirement. Women who get their insurance from these exempt "religious employers" will have insurance policies that do not cover contraception.

Other non-profit organizations with religious affiliations are offered an "accommodation" to the requirement. Under the accommodation, these entities can opt-out of covering contraception in their employer- or school-based health policies. The objecting entity can take advantage of the accommodation by filling out a form that serves as notice of its religious objection. The insurer then removes contraception from the nonprofit's health plan. Federal rules make the insurer financially responsible for the employees' contraception. (For an overview of this issue, see the Sept/Oct 2015 issue of the WHA, "What to Do If Your Employer Is a Religious Refuser.") (The Supreme Court addressed challenges to the contraceptive coverage requirement by for-profit employers in 2014.)

Yet—despite the numerous allowances the government has made to address the employers' religious beliefs—the non-profits bringing these lawsuits remain unsatisfied. They object to even providing notice of their objection, arguing that doing so makes them "complicit" in facilitating contraceptive coverage. Their lawsuits claim that the accommodation violates the Religious

Freedom and Restoration Act, a Federal statute that says the government cannot "substantially burden a person's exercise of religion" unless the government's action "is the least restrictive means" of furthering a "compelling government interest."[7]

The government maintains that the notification requirement is not burdensome. By filling out a form, an objecting employer can relieve itself of any obligation to cover contraception. Instead, the government uses its authority to ensure that women receive contraception through a third-party insurer or administrator.

If these challenges are successful, employers could make it difficult, perhaps even impossible, for women to obtain and/or use health insurance coverage for contraception. Employers would be allowed to impose their beliefs on women, and could create a situation where their employees simply cannot afford to access contraception, increasing their likelihood of unintended pregnancy.

To date, 8 out of 9 Federal appellate courts that have considered challenges to the accommodation have disagreed with the non-profits and have upheld it.[8] The Eighth Circuit is the only circuit to have sided with the non-profits.

If the Supreme Court splits 4-4, it could decide to let the lower court rulings stand, creating a legal patchwork across the country. Women would likely have coverage of essential contraceptive care in every state in the U.S., unless they live within the Eighth Circuit (Arkansas, Iowa, Minnesota, Missouri, and Nebraska). Because there are still dozens of other similar lawsuits still pending, however, the issue will likely find its way back to the Court in the future. Alternatively, as with *Whole Woman's Health*, if the Court splits 4-4, it could decide to defer a decision.

If, on the other hand, Justice Kennedy sides with the liberal justices, he would provide the decisive fifth vote to uphold the accommodation, setting nationwide precedent (and, hopefully, laying this issue to rest for once and for all).

A lot is at stake for women: the right to receive abortion and contraceptive care and to make their own health care decisions. These cases underscore the pivotal role that the Supreme Court plays in our lives. And, Justice Scalia's death raises the stakes of the 2016 presidential election.

1. How would you side in the HB 2 case?

2. Do you think the non-profits challenging the Affordable Care Act (ACA) have a valid case, or are they overreaching based on ideology? Explain your position.

CHAPTER 4

WHAT ADVOCACY GROUPS SAY

A significant portion of the battle for public influence on abortion takes place on the advocacy front. Predictably, both pro-choice and anti-abortion advocates claim the moral high ground: pro-choice supporters focus on the undue expense, inconvenience, and societal disapproval women seeking abortions must face. Those on the pro-life side claim that abortion is murdering a human life, and should be banned in most cases.

While both sides inspire passionate feelings, anti-abortion groups arguably go further to actualize their beliefs. Signs depicting fetuses, gravestones for the unborn, and other similarly lurid graphic representations are used to stir the emotions. To defend the absolutist position that abortion is murder, anti-abortionists sometimes advance spurious claims. For example, despite the assertion that abortion leads to higher rates of breast cancer, no such link has even been substantiated in any credible peer-reviewed study. In several states, new laws mandate that abortion seekers be exposed to insufficiently proven information regarding physical and psychological risk factors. Finally, those who work in abortion clinics report receiving threats of violence from those on the extreme fringes of the pro-life movement. Since pro-lifers view abortion as inherently violent, these extremists perhaps feel justified in carrying out threats to those doing their job. Nonetheless, under the law, a threat of violence in the workplace is considered harassment.

In this chapter, we will take a look at what a few of the leading pro-choice and anti-abortion advocacy groups have to say. On the pro-choice side, National Abortion and Reproductive Rights Action League (NARAL) presents a convincing case that restrictions to abortion endanger women. We'll also take a look inside the Susan Thompson Buffett Foundation, one of the wealthiest supporters of women's reproductive rights. On the pro-life side, Clarke Forsythe lays out his recommendations of how our next president can advance this agenda. Much power to do so lies in judicial nominations, so this is a key area of interest for observers of the reproductive rights debate.

"ABORTION BANS ENDANGER WOMEN'S HEALTH," FROM NATIONAL ABORTION AND REPRODUCTIVE RIGHTS ACTION LEAGUE (NARAL)

Roe v. Wade stands as a milestone to women's freedom and equality, and one of its most fundamental tenets is that a woman's health must always be protected. Yet 40 years after the Supreme Court recognized the right to choose and the vital importance of women's health,[1] attacks on women's privacy, and on health protections in particular, continue. Time after time, anti-choice lawmakers vote down proposed health exceptions to abortion restrictions,[2] and prominent anti-choice leaders openly state their opposition to protecting women's health.[3] And perhaps most ominously, with the addition of George W. Bush's appointees Chief Justice John Roberts and Justice Samuel Alito to the U.S. Supreme Court, the balance on the nation's highest court has shifted.[4] The court's opinion in the jointly decided cases of *Gonzales v. Planned Parenthood Federation of America* and *Gonzales v. Carhart* [5] offers insight into *Roe's* fate. These two cases challenged the Federal Abortion Ban, a nationwide ban that, as written, could have outlawed abortion as early as the 12th week in pregnancy but, as interpreted somewhat more narrowly by the court, outlaws a second-trimester abortion method, one that doctors have said is necessary to protect some women's health.[6] Startlingly, this ban has no health exception.[7] By upholding the federal ban in *Carhart*, the court retreated from more than four decades of precedent that ensured a woman's health must always be protected. Future decisions based on this new precedent may further undermine *Roe* and endanger women's health.

THE SUPREME COURT HAS LONG RECOGNIZED THE IMPORTANCE OF PROTECTING WOMEN'S HEALTH

- *Roe v. Wade (1973):*[8] By a vote of 7-2, the Supreme Court invalidated a Texas law that prohibited abortion in all cases except when necessary to save a woman's life. The court placed great emphasis on women's health, holding that after the first trimester a state may regulate abortion to promote women's health, and that after fetal viability, abortion may be regulated or prohibited only if there are exceptions to protect the woman's life and health.
- *Doe v. Bolton (1973):*[9] Decided with *Roe v. Wade*, *Doe* invalidated provisions of Georgia's very restrictive abortion law. The law included among other requirements that a woman secure the approval of three physicians and a hospital committee before she could obtain abortion care. The court held that a physician's decision to provide abortion services must rest upon "his best clinical judgment," which includes all factors relevant to the woman's health, including physical condition, mental health, psychological condition, family circumstances, and age.
- *Planned Parenthood of Southeastern Pennsylvania v. Casey (1992):*[10] By a narrow 5-4 vote, the court reaffirmed *Roe v. Wade's* essential holdings, including the centrality of women's health. The court recognized a

woman's right to choose abortion before viability without undue interference from the state. This decision affirmed a state's right to restrict abortion services after fetal viability but required that any restrictions include exceptions to protect a woman's life and health.

- ***Stenberg v. Carhart (2000):***[11] By a slim 5-4 majority, the Supreme Court held unconstitutional Nebraska's ban that outlawed abortion care as early as the 12th week of pregnancy (a ban on so-called "partial-birth" abortion). The court struck down the law in large part because it had no exception for women's health. The court clarified that the health exception must protect women against health risks caused by the pregnancy as well as health risks caused by a regulation that forces a doctor to choose a less medically appropriate procedure. "[A] risk to a woman's health is the same whether it happens to arise from regulating a particular method of abortion, or from barring abortion entirely."[12] The court explicitly recognized that "the absence of a health exception will place women at an unnecessary risk of tragic health consequences."[13]

- ***Ayotte v. Planned Parenthood (2006):*** The Supreme Court accepted this case to review two questions, one relating to the requirement of health exceptions in laws restricting abortion.[14] Specifically, the court agreed to consider the question of whether a parental-notification law requires a medical emergency provision. The case was decided largely on technical grounds and returned to the lower courts for a final decision, but the court did restate its precedent that the government may not endanger women's health when regulating abortion services: "New Hampshire does not dispute, and our precedents hold, that a State may not restrict access to abortions that are 'necessary, in appropriate medical judgment, for preservation of the life or health of the mother.'"[15] (While the lower court was considering the remanded case, New Hampshire legislators repealed the parental-notification law at issue, rendering the remaining issue moot.[16] Unfortunately, several years later the New Hampshire legislature reenacted the law; it is now in force and does not have a fully adequate exception to protect young women's health.[17])

RECONFIGURED COURT WITH BUSH APPOINTEES REVERSES PRECEDENT

Though for 40 years the court has respected the sanctity of protections for women's health recognized in *Roe*, with its decision to uphold the Federal Abortion Ban, the Supreme Court held that the government may force a woman to undergo a more dangerous medical procedure than the one her doctor would have recommended.

- *Gonzales v. Planned Parenthood Federation of America and Gonzales v. Carhart (2007):* The Supreme Court voted 5-4 to uphold the Federal Abortion Ban, a measure that outlaws certain second-trimester abortions and has no exception for cases when a woman's health is in danger. Reversing course from their earlier decision in Stenberg which found unconstitutional a similar state ban in Nebraska, the justices reasoned that other procedures are available to women who would have undergone the banned procedure.[18] The court's majority opinion also cited its unfounded concern that a woman might regret her choice to terminate a pregnancy as a reason for banning the doctor's recommended procedure, without offering a legal explanation as to how this concern justified endangering her own health or the health of other women for whom the procedure might be a medical necessity.[19] Perhaps most ominously, President Bush's appointees to the court cast the critical votes to uphold the ban, signaling the first time the court has turned its back on *Roe's* core holding safeguarding women's health.

LEGAL ABORTION CAN SAVE WOMEN'S LIVES AND SAFEGUARD WOMEN'S HEALTH

Any regulation of abortion care must recognize the full range of health risks pregnant women face. Indeed, a clear majority of Americans believe that abortion must remain safe and legal to protect a woman's health and safety.[20]

Many women welcome pregnancy and can look forward to a safe childbirth; however, for some, pregnancy can be medically risky. Abortion restrictions that have no exceptions to protect women's health are dangerous. Without health exceptions, women who have high-risk pregnancies would be forced to continue the pregnancy at the expense of their own health and sometimes lives:

- Vikki Stella, a diabetic, discovered during her 32nd week of pregnancy that the fetus she was carrying suffered from several major anomalies and had no chance of survival. Because of Vikki's diabetes, her doctor determined that induced labor and Caesarian section were both riskier procedures for Vikki than an abortion. The procedure not only protected Vikki from immediate medical risks, but also ensured that she would be able to have children in the future.[21]

- Jennifer Peterson was 35 and pregnant when she discovered a lump in her breast. Tests showed she had invasive breast cancer.[22] The cancer and its treatment, separate and apart from the pregnancy, were a threat to her health. A health exception recognizes the added threat to her health posed by pregnancy during the onset and treatment of her cancer, while without such an exception Jennifer would have been forced to continue her dangerous pregnancy. About one in 3,000 pregnant women also has breast cancer during her pregnancy, and for these women, a health exception is absolutely necessary.[23]

- Beth Whalen, a 40-year-old mother of one, was diagnosed with heart disease after the birth of her son. She learned that any subsequent pregnancy could shave 10 years off her life.[24] Without a health exception that considers the risk that pregnancy poses to Beth's long-term survival, Beth and women like her would be forced to carry dangerous pregnancies to term.

- Doctors report that many pregnant women with heart-valve disorders die each year from blood clots which, absent pregnancy, would not be life threatening.[25] A physician who specializes in maternal cardiac medicine said that there are "extreme pregnancy-associated risks" for women with these heart conditions. The doctor explained: "A high risk of maternal mortality has implications not just for the mother but also for any potential baby and siblings at home. And even if she survives the pregnancy, the woman may have a reduced life expectancy or suffer from limited physical capacity."[26] For a woman presenting late in a pregnancy with a severe heart disorder, a health exception recognizes the totality of the risks she faces and allows her to make the best decision for her health, her life, and her family.

A health exception also must account for the mental-health problems that may occur in pregnancy. Severe fetal anomalies, for example, can exact a tremendous emotional toll on a pregnant woman and her family.

- Danielle Deaver was 22 weeks pregnant when her water broke. Tests showed that Danielle had suffered anhydramnios, a premature rupture of the membranes before the fetus has achieved viability. Without sufficient amniotic fluid, the fetus likely would be born with a shortening of muscle tissue that results in the inability to move limbs. In addition, the fetus likely would suffer deformities to the face and head, and the lungs were unlikely to develop beyond the 22-week point. The couple, in counsel with their doctor, explored every possible action to save the pregnancy. However, there was less than a 10-percent chance that, if born, the baby would be able to breathe on its own and only a two-percent chance the baby would be able to eat on its own. They decided to terminate the pregnancy, but care was unavailable because an abortion ban in their state lacked a health exception. Eight days later, after Danielle endured intense pain and infection, their daughter Elizabeth was born and survived for just 15 minutes.[27]
- Christy Zink was 21 weeks pregnant when she learned the fetus she was carrying was suffering from multiple severe anomalies including agenesis of the

corpus callosum—a rare birth defect in which the central connecting structure of the brain is absent. Even more severe, the brain had developed in small globular splotches, meaning effectively that an entire hemisphere of the brain was missing. Christy and her husband consulted medical experts around the world and were told that, if the fetus survived the pregnancy, which was uncertain, the baby would be in a state of near-constant seizures, requiring numerous surgeries to remove what little of the brain matter remained. Christy made the decision to terminate the pregnancy, a difficult, but critical choice that a health exception must protect for all women.[28]

- During the seventh month of Coreen Costello's third pregnancy, her doctors determined that her fetus was suffering from a lethal neurological disorder. Because of their profound religious beliefs, the Costellos wanted to undergo a natural delivery process, but after Coreen's health worsened, her doctors discovered that the head was too large to fit through Coreen's cervix; a traditional delivery would have cost Coreen her fertility. After much anguish, Coreen accepted her physician's recommendation that an abortion was the most appropriate option for her. She later stated: "Because of the safety of this procedure ... I can have another healthy baby."[29]

- When two doctors confirmed that, among other ailments, Tammy Watts' fetus had no eyes and extensive internal organ abnormalities including kidneys that were already failing, Tammy and her husband recognized that their much-wanted child would never survive.[30] After her experience, Tammy said: "You can't take this away from women and families. You can't. It's so important that we be able to make these decisions, because we're the only ones who can."[31]

- Because Viki Wilson's fetus suffered from encephalocoele, two-thirds of its brain had formed outside its skull and it tragically would not survive. A traditional birthing process would have not only further harmed the fetus, but likely would have ruptured Viki's uterus as well. Her doctor also determined that a Caesarean section would be too dangerous. An abortion was the safest solution for Viki, who called the procedure their "salvation."[32]

ANTI-CHOICE ACTIVISTS AND LAWMAKERS REJECT EXCEPTIONS TO PROTECT A WOMAN'S LIFE:

"There is never a reason in law or in practice to advocate a 'life of the mother' exception for abortion."

-- American Life League

Declaration: Protecting the Life of the Mother, at http://www.all.org/article.php?id=10681&search=doctors (emphasis added) (last visited Nov. 3, 2014).

"In present-day practice of obstetrics in this country, having to choose between the life of one [woman] and the life of the other [fetus] as a practical matter that just doesn't come up. It just doesn't."

-- Rep. Michael Burgess (R-TX)

Protect Life Ac: Hearing on H.R.358 Before the House Energy and Commerce Subcomm. on Health, 112th Cong. (2011).

"With modern technology and science, you can't find one instance [of abortion necessary to save a woman's life] ... There is no such exception as life of the mother, and as far as health of the mother, same thing."

-- Rep. Joe Walsh (R-IL)

Walsh, Duckworth Clash on Medicare, Abortion, at http://articles.chicagotribune.com/2012-10- 18/news/chi-walsh -duckworth-clash-onmedicare-abortion-20121018_1 _democraticchallenger-tammy-duckworth-walsh-abortionrights abortion-rights

ELIMINATING THE HEALTH EXCEPTION IS AN ANTI-CHOICE TACTIC TO DISMANTLE *ROE*

Anti-choice activists already succeeded in changing the legal standards for assessing restrictions on a woman's right to choose; in *Casey* (1992), the court abandoned the most exacting standard of legal review applied to fundamental rights, "strict scrutiny," and instead implemented the less protective standard of asking merely whether a restriction imposes an "undue burden" on a woman's right to choose.[33] A second avenue of attack on *Roe* is to restrict or eliminate altogether its protections for women's health. Anti-choice activists consider the protection of women's health to be a "loophole" that must be closed. As they see it, eliminating the health exception would destroy another pillar of *Roe* and make further attacks on the core right to legal abortion more likely to succeed.

* Anti-choice activists fought for more than a decade to outlaw safe, pre-viability, second-trimester abortion

methods without an exception to protect a woman's health. With the Supreme Court's decision in *Carhart* to uphold the Federal Abortion Ban – a case in which President Bush's anti-choice appointees Chief Justice John Roberts and Justice Samuel Alito cast decisive votes against women's health – the anti-choice movement had its first significant Supreme Court victory in 15 years, and arguably made its biggest step yet toward overturning *Roe* and eliminating constitutional protection for women's health in the abortion context.[34]

- Anti-choice activists lobbied for years for state abortion bans similar to the Federal Abortion Ban. Of the 30 states with laws on the books banning safe and medically appropriate abortion procedures (so-called "partial-birth" abortion bans),[35] 29 have absolutely no health exception.[36] Most of these laws are unconstitutional and unenforceable as written due to the court's 2000 decision in *Stenberg*. As a result of the court's 2007 decision in *Carhart*, however, many states seized the opportunity to enact abortion bans without appropriate health exceptions, despite the existence of the nationwide ban. In addition, women have been robbed of federal protections from overreaching state laws previously found within the judicial system. In the wake of *Carhart*, the Supreme Court remanded a case enjoining Virginia's abortion ban back to a lower court for reconsideration. While the court had previously found the ban unconstitutional, in 2009 in *Herring v. Richmond Med. Ctr. for Women,* the Fourth Circuit Court of Appeals allowed the law to go into effect.[37]

- Anti-choice activists admit that "inducing the Court to define 'health' in a restrictive manner represent[s] a beneficial strategy in reversing *Roe.*"[38] Now, five sitting justices on the Supreme Court have made clear their hostility to the health exception as originally established in *Roe* and *Doe.*

CONCLUSION

The Supreme Court long articulated that abortion regulations must protect a woman's health. Then President Bush reconfigured the court and within months it reversed course. In the meantime, anti-choice activists continue to press for abortion restrictions that endanger women's health and put their safety at risk. American women are relying on lawmakers and courts to reject such dangerous and unwise proposals.

January 1, 2016

1. With so many complex potential risk factors facing pregnant women, do you think that the legal system has any business regulating the specifics of abortion? Or should that be left to doctors?

2. Based on what we have read up to this point, are there signs that lawmakers and courts will reject abortion restrictions?

"ACTIVISTS PURSUE PRIVATE ABORTION DETAILS USING PUBLIC RECORDS LAWS," BY CHARLES ORNSTEIN, FROM *PROPUBLICA*, AUGUST 25, 2015

THIS STORY WAS CO-PUBLISHED WITH THE WASHINGTON POST.

Across the country, those who support abortion rights and those who oppose them are feuding in court over how much information should be disclosed about women undergoing abortions. Supporters say there's no margin for error. Opponents say it's about ensuring quality care.

A few years back, Jonathan Bloedow filed a series of requests under Washington state's Public Records Act asking for details on pregnancies terminated at abortion clinics around the state. For every abortion, he wanted information on the woman's age and race, where she lived, how long she had been pregnant and how past pregnancies had ended. He also wanted to know about any complications, but he didn't ask for names. This is all information that Washington's health department, as those in other states, collects to track vital statistics.

Bloedow, 43, isn't a public health researcher, a traditional journalist or a clinic owner. He's an anti-abortion activist who had previously sued Planned Parenthood, accusing the group of overcharging the government for contraception.

"There are stories in the data that bring home the reality of what these people do," Bloedow, a software engineer, said in an email. "Any good investigator knows that when you're dealing with hard-core criminals, if you 'keep crawling through their garbage' some evidence of criminality and corruption will turn up."

The health department had already given him data for one provider, he said, and was on the verge of turning over more information when Planned Parenthood and other clinics sued, arguing that releasing the records would violate health department rules and privacy laws.

The legal skirmish, and others like it nationwide, reveal a quiet evolution in the nation's abortion battle. Increasingly, abortion opponents are pursuing personal and medical information on women undergoing abortions and the doctors who perform them. They often file complaints with authorities based on what they learn.

Abortion opponents insist their tactics are generally not aimed at identifying women who have abortions but to uncover incidents involving patients who may have been harmed by poor care or underage girls who may have been sexually abused. They say they are trying to prevent situations such as the one involving Philadelphia abortion doctor Kermit Gosnell, who was convicted in 2013 of murdering three babies after botched abortions and of involuntary manslaughter in the death of a woman.

"This is about saving the lives of women," said Cheryl Sullenger, senior policy adviser for the anti-abortion group Operation Rescue, which is based in Wichita, Kansas. "A lot of people don't understand that. It's a systemic problem within the abortion industry today for abortion providers to cut corners on patient care."

But those who support abortion rights say the ultimate aim of these activists is to reduce abortions by intimidating women and their doctors — using the loss of privacy as a weapon. They say their opponents are amassing a wealth of details that could be used to identify patients — turning women, and their doctors, into pariahs or even targets. In a

New Mexico case, a woman's initials and where she lived became public as part of an investigation triggered by a complaint from activists.

"I don't think there's any margin for error here," said Laura Einstein, chief legal counsel of Planned Parenthood of the Great Northwest and the Hawaiian Islands, which challenged Bloedow's request. "These women came to a private health center to have a private health procedure, and that's just not anybody's business."

In recent years, abortion opponents have become experts at accessing public records such as recordings of 911 calls, autopsy reports and documents from state health departments and medical boards, then publishing the information on their websites.

Some activists have dug through clinics' trash to find privacy violations by abortion providers — such as patient records tossed in dumpsters — and used them to file complaints with regulators.

The fight has landed in courts nationwide as the two sides tussle over which information about abortions should be public and which should remain confidential under privacy laws.

In St. Louis, for example, an Operation Rescue staff member is suing the city's fire department for 911 call logs and recordings from a Planned Parenthood clinic. The city says releasing the requested information would violate a federal patient privacy law.

In Louisiana, a critic of abortion sued the state last year to get data on abortions performed on minors, their ages and the ages of the listed biological fathers, as well as any complications that occurred. The state said the records were exempt from disclosure, and a judge agreed.

In Bloedow's case, a Washington court sided with the clinics and prohibited the release of the records he sought. In May, a state appeals court upheld that injunction.

"The public has no legitimate interest in the health care or pregnancy history of any individual woman or where any particular abortion was performed," the appeals court ruled.

A TUSSLE OVER PRIVACY

At its core, the Supreme Court's 1973 decision in *Roe v. Wade* rested on the right to privacy. The court determined that this right — guaranteed under the due process clause of the 14th Amendment — extended to a woman's decision to have an abortion.

With the 1996 passage of the Health Insurance Portability and Accountability Act, known as HIPAA, additional federal privacy protections took hold for patients.

When Planned Parenthood officials were recently caught on video discussing the sale of donated fetal tissue, the organization invoked the potential violations of patient privacy to protest the surreptitious filming.

Still, the extent of the privacy guaranteed to those who seek abortions has been tested repeatedly.

In 2003, after Congress passed the Partial-Birth Abortion Ban, abortion providers sued to challenge its constitutionality. The Justice Department, as part of its defense of the law, sought patient records from a Chicago hospital, where a doctor was one of the plaintiffs' expert witnesses.

Though patients' names would have been redacted, a federal appeals court denied the request, citing privacy concerns.

"Imagine if nude pictures of a woman, uploaded to the Internet without her consent though without identifying her by name, were downloaded in a foreign country by people who will never meet her," the court wrote. "She would still feel that her privacy had been invaded. The revelation of the intimate details contained in the record of a late-term abortion may inflict a similar wound."

Around the same time, at least two state attorneys general, both abortion opponents, pressed for similar patient records. The attorney general of Kansas succeeded in part, while his counterpart in Indiana failed.

DIGGING FOR DIRT

More recently, it has been activists like Sullenger and Bloedow seeking information about abortion providers and their patients.

Coast to coast, they appear to be drawing from an unofficial playbook: Some wait outside clinics, tracking or taking photos of patients' and staffers' license plates and ambulances, if called.

They not only mine public records but also collect information leaked by sympathetic health care workers — for example, emergency-room doctors and ambulance drivers — who are required to keep patient information confidential under HIPAA. The law, however, doesn't apply to advocacy groups.

Sullenger acknowledges receiving private patient information and said it helps to confirm when patients have suffered complications or died. In most cases, she said, the group does not name patients or publish photographs of them.

(Sullenger served two years in federal prison for conspiring to bomb a California abortion clinic in the 1980s. Today, the Operation Rescue website says, she denounces violence.)

The leaked information is used by activists to bolster complaints they submit to health agencies against abortion providers, sometimes without patients' knowledge. Operation Rescue estimates that it has 100 complaints currently pending in different states.

Sullenger said it shouldn't be left solely to patients to bring such matters forward. "If someone else sees that there may be an issue, we have a public duty to report things like that."

Sometimes, complaints have brought violations to light.

In Indiana, the group Right to Life obtained thousands of pregnancy termination reports from the state health department. The records are nearly identical to those requested by Bloedow in Washington, but Indiana granted the request, redacting only a few fields.

After analyzing the data, the group filed a litany of complaints with the state, alleging that doctors were violating abortion record-keeping laws, including failure to report abortions involving minors in a timely manner. Four physicians now face disciplinary proceedings.

Such cases can be pursued without violating the privacy of patients, said Cathie Humbarger, vice president of policy enforcement for Indiana Right to Life. "We're not aware of one situation where someone identified a patient by looking at a termination of pregnancy report after it was released by the state," Humbarger said in an email sent through a spokeswoman.

One Indiana doctor, who has acknowledged making an "honest mistake" involving paperwork, faces a misdemeanor criminal charge.

His attorneys have argued that he did not knowingly violate the law and unsuccessfully sought to have the medical board case dismissed before a hearing.

But there have been other instances in which anti-abortion groups have filed unfounded complaints, said Janet Crepps, a senior counsel for the Center for Reproductive Rights. The resulting investigations caused additional details about the patients to be made public, she said.

Operation Rescue and another group filed complaints with New Mexico's medical board against a doctor who works at an Albuquerque clinic after a patient experienced a complication and was taken to a hospital, and they obtained a recording of the 911 call.

Though the board ultimately exonerated the doctor, many details about the patient — her age and her mental state, in addition to her initials and where she lived — came out in a transcript of a hearing.

"The woman clearly did not want her privacy violated," said Vicki Saporta, chief executive of the National Abortion Federation, a professional association for abortion providers. "She didn't want to talk to anybody."

AFTER A DEATH, ALL BETS ARE OFF

Anti-abortion groups typically tread carefully when it comes to living patients.

Operation Rescue's website in March published a photograph of a woman being wheeled out of a St. Louis clinic on a stretcher but put a black bar over her eyes to obscure her identity.

When a patient dies, however, it can be a different story.

In 2013, a different abortion opponent wrote on her blog that an "impeccable informant" told her the identity of a kindergarten teacher who had died after a late-term abortion at a clinic in Germantown, Maryland. Groups including Operation Rescue quickly got the word out, using the woman's name and photos from social-media sites.

The doctor who performed the abortion, LeRoy Carhart, has been a target for protesters because he does late-term abortions that most other practitioners won't. Though abortion opponents blame him for the woman's death, the Maryland medical board found no deficiencies in his care for her.

Saporta said the woman's family did not authorize the release of her identity.

Sullenger said she sympathized with the family's loss but not its demand for privacy. "Look, once a person dies, they don't have any privacy anymore," she said. "I think they should have been more concerned about it happening to another person."

Contacted recently, the woman's mother declined to comment.

'ALL THEY CARED ABOUT WAS JUDGING ME'

For some patients, the grief they already feel with the end of a pregnancy is compounded by the loss of privacy.

Alicia, who spoke on the condition that only her first name be used, had an abortion in November 2013 after her OB/GYN told her and her husband that the fetus had a severe form of spina bifida, a debilitating birth defect.

During the procedure, she began bleeding heavily from a tear in her uterus. The clinic, located in Bellevue, south of Omaha, summoned an ambulance, which took Alicia to the hospital.

Someone protesting outside the clinic took a photo of the ambulance, and Operation Rescue's website reported the incident, though it did not know Alicia's identity.

Within weeks, the Nebraska health department subpoenaed Alicia's records from the clinic. Alicia had not complained, but the agency had received a tip, she later learned.

"All this happened because I was in the clinic having a legal abortion," she said. "All they cared about was judging me ... and building evidence for their case."

Alicia said while the complication was scary at the time, it had been explained to her in advance as a possibility. She said she didn't blame her doctor, Carhart, who practices in Nebraska as well as in Maryland.

In an interview, Carhart said that several of his patients have had their privacy violated.

After subpoenaing Alicia's records, Nebraska's health department disciplined a nurse at Carhart's clinic for a pattern of negligence and unprofessional conduct involving a dozen patients, including Alicia.

Alicia said she asked state officials to identify who had filed the complaint that provided her name to state officials. To her amazement, she was told that information was confidential.

Marla Augustine, a health department spokeswoman, said in an email that patients are not notified if their records are examined "to protect the process from being contaminated." For instance, a patient so notified could tip off a health provider about the existence of an investigation. That said, Augustine added: "The confidentiality of a patient's medical records is very important to us, and a paramount consideration."

Her explanation provides little comfort to Alicia.

"I don't understand why whoever did this gets to be anonymous while I was the one who was supposed to not have my information leaked," she said. "Why does that person get more rights than me?"

1. How do you balance the right to gather information with the right to privacy? Do you think patients' privacy should be protected at all costs? Or do you think private information should circulate, as long as it is anonymous?

2. What if the article above was about pro-choice advocates seeking private information for research to expand reproductive rights? Would the balance between privacy and expanded rights and freedom change at all then, in your opinion?

"WHO'S WHO AT THE SECRETIVE SUSAN THOMPSON BUFFETT FOUNDATION?" BY DAVID CALLAHAN, FROM *INSIDE PHILANTHROPY*, FEBRUARY 4, 2014

Want to ruin a perfectly a nice day at the office? Try to identify someone to pitch at the Susan Thompson Buffett Foundation. The place is a case study in non-transparency, and it's super hard to even figure out who's doing the grantmaking. Which is crazy, because putting aside medical foundations that assist patients, STBF ranked number five in total giving in 2012, shelling out $367.1 million in 2012. That total put it well ahead of such brand name biggies as Robert Wood Johnson, Kellogg, Open Society Foundations, Mellon, and Packard.

For most grantseekers, trying to penetrate this place is like being a tourist asking around for the Mafia in Little Italy. The website is a laughable dead end, focusing only on STBF's education giving while omitting huge key funding areas, and STBF's 990s lag maddeningly behind by a few years. If you try calling the foundation, you get a message saying that nobody is there and that they don't accept proposals, have funding guidelines, or publish an annual report (but at least you can leave a message!).

While you can understand why a foundation that is deeply enmeshed in protecting abortion rights might want to keep a low profile, this seems excessive.

We all know that STBF is moving big money in developing countries and also here in the United States. But to whom, and why, and through what grantmaking programs with what priorities run by what staff—all that is quite mysterious.

Until now.

Okay, I'm overpromising. But I'll do my best to shed some light on STBF by explaining who's giving out all that money. Once I'm done, I'll have written the longest article I know of about one of the biggest spending foundations in the world, which says something about the state of media coverage of philanthropy.

Warren Buffett established the foundation, originally named the Buffett Foundation, in the 1960s. It was renamed the Susan Thompson Buffett Foundation in honor of his wife after her death in 2004.

For a long time, the foundation gave away lots of money, but not compared to Buffett's fortune. Susan was the foundation's president, and Warren tended to stay out of things. The foundation focused mainly on the couple's shared concerns about reproductive rights and population control. Big gifts were made annually to a relatively small number of groups, including Planned Parenthood and International Projects Assistance Services.

Allen Greenberg, then married to the Buffetts' daughter Susan, was put in charge of the foundation's operations in 1987 and, for years, was the foundation's only employee. He still serves as executive director. More about him in a moment.

The foundation suddenly became a very big deal when Susan Buffett died and left it around $2.5 billion. Overnight, it joined the ranks of the top 25 or so foundations in the United States. It stepped up its giving dramatically.

And the foundation's assets are slated to keep growing, due to a planned infusion of Berkshire Hathaway shares from Warren worth several billion dollars over coming years. STBF could easily double in size.

Even as its giving expanded, though, the foundation has remained very much a family affair. **Susan Buffett**, or Susie, is the board chair. Peter Buffett is also on the board, or was as of 2012. Greenberg is still ED, as I said, and serves on the board, too, with a handful of other people.

Susie appears to be a driving force behind the foundation's giving, even as she also runs her own Sherwood Foundation. Susie is into lots of issues, both domestic and international. She's been deeply concerned about global development issues, and both she and her brother, Howard G. Buffett, are on the board of ONE, the global anti-poverty organization co-founded by Bono.

I can (and will) write a whole long post about Susie, who is a very low-profile funder. But suffice to say that she appears to be the most pivotal figure in the STBF universe.

Greenberg has really made the foundation his life's work, and there are no signs that will change as he approaches 60. For somebody overseeing such big giving, he keeps a remarkably low profile. You won't find any media interviews with him, or see him on panels at foundation conferences. As a result, it's hard to know what he thinks about anything.

What we do know about Greenberg is that he's a lawyer and used to work at Public Citizen, the progressive watchdog group founded by Ralph Nader. After moving to Omaha to run the foundation, Greenberg worked closely with Susan Thompson Buffett when she was alive, and earned the respect of the NGOs they were supporting in the family planning space.

The next two key figures at the foundation are **Türkiz Gökgöl,** who directs its international program, and **Tracy Weitz**, who directs the domestic program.

Gökgöl is incredibly low profile, given how much money STBF gives out internationally. (Notice a pattern here?) Again, no media interviews, no long bio on LinkedIn, no ubiquity on the conference circuit. Gökgöl is originally from Turkey, but earned her doctorate from Harvard University in 1979. She then became a professor before joining Pathfinder International in 1983 as its representative in Turkey. She stayed with that organization into the 1990s, becoming its vice president for Asia and Near East, and expanding the group's work on family planning and reproductive health into several new countries. She also did a stint at the UNFPA in the late 1990s running its operations in the former Soviet republics of Central Asia.

Coming back to Turkey, she started a reproductive rights organization called the Willows Foundation in late 1990s, and was involved in other Turkish groups as well, working in tough terrain to empower women. Presumably, this is how she hooked up with STBF, where she started working in 2005.

You won't find email addresses for any of the program officers on the foundation's website, but here's Gökgöl's: tgokgol@stbfoundation.org.

Tracy Weitz, on the domestic side of STBF, is brand new in this job—no press release, of course—which she took over from Judith De Sarno, a long time leader on reproductive rights issues.

Weitz is another impressive scholar-practitioner, with a PhD in medical sociology and a master's in public administration. She worked for Planned Parenthood early in her career, and she's worked squarely on abortion and women's health issues for many years at the University of California in San Francisco, where she's been affiliated since 2002. Her bio at USCF states:

Dr. Weitz's passion is for those aspects of women's health which are marginalized either for ideological reasons, or because the populations affected lack the means or mechanisms to have their concerns raised. Her current research focuses on innovative strategies to expand abortion provision in the U.S. Included in her research portfolio is a demonstration project of the use of nurse practitioners, certified nurse midwives, and physician assistants as providers of abortion care in California, several studies of abortion regulation, and a national strategic plan to secure access to later abortion care.

Sounds like the right person to be heading up STBF's domestic work, which has long taken the foundation into the heart of the abortion battle. Weitz's USCF email is is weitzt@obgyn.ucsf.edu. Her email at STBF, we presume, is tweitz@stbfoundation.org.

I could go further down the list of STBF staff, but this post is pretty long already. However, if search the foundation's name on LinkedIn, you'll find a bunch of them, including **Stephen Heartwell**, the deputy director of domestic programs (sheartwell@stbfoundation.org), program officers like **Lindsey Barari** and **Karen Gluck** (kgluck@stbfoundation.org), **Kellie Pickett**, Director of Scholarships (kpickett@stbfoundation.org), and others.

1. Why does the author claim that the Susan Thompson Buffett Foundation (STBF) is overly secretive? Do you agree?

2. Given the controversial nature of their abortion rights advocacy work, do you think more transparency would be a good idea for STBF?

"HOW THE NEXT PRESIDENT CAN PROTECT HUMAN LIFE," BY CLARKE FORSYTHE, FROM THE *NATIONAL REVIEW ONLINE*, JUNE 20, 2016

When Donald Trump commented that "the laws are set" on abortion, he articulated a profound misunderstanding of the legal realities of the issue and the impact they will have on the next president of the United States. The laws on abortion have not been "set" since the Supreme Court nationalized the issue with its 1973 edict in *Roe v. Wade*. And, in fact, the Obama administration has spent the past seven years federalizing matters of life through Obamacare and other administrative maneuvers, and doing what it can to thwart health and safety standards that protect women and to increase taxpayer funding for abortion. There is much a President Trump could and should do to do to reverse this disastrous course, and conservative leaders must make that clear during their much-anticipated meeting with him in New York on Tuesday.

Here is a short list of ways an engaged president could protect life.

THE SUPREME COURT & FEDERAL JUDICIAL APPOINTMENTS

The nomination of Supreme Court justices is among the most consequential powers a president has, as the current dispute over Merrick Garland proves. The next president will, for better or worse, shape the Supreme Court for the next quarter century. By next January, three of the eight sitting justices will be 80 or nearly 80, meaning that, along with the vacancy left by Antonin Scalia's death, the next president may ultimately appoint as many as four justices.

The essential issue at stake is protecting self-government: When the Supreme Court goes beyond enforcing the Constitution as understood by its text, structure, and history, and takes policy issues away from the people, the right of self-government is stolen. The cause of life is best served when law and policy are left to the democratic process rather than being hijacked by the courts, because the American people increasingly support the protection of human life, especially at the state level.

It is long past time for the Supreme Court to return the issue of abortion to the states by overturning the reckless *Roe* decision, which legalized abortion for any reason at any time of pregnancy in all 50 states, isolating the U.S. as one of only four nations — out of 195 around the globe — that allow abortion in all circumstances after fetal viability. As documented by poll after poll, and the action of state after state over the past decade, the American people clearly want fewer abortions. And yet the Court seems poised to stamp out state limits and health and safety regulations that are supported by the majority of voters, perpetuating the issue rather than resolving it.

FIVE-MONTH LIMIT ON ABORTIONS

Common-sense limits on abortion have been stymied by the threat of vetoes by President Obama. These limitations are supported by a majority of Americans and should be signed by the next president.

Last year, for example, the U.S. House passed a prohibition on abortion after five months. The bill also received a majority vote in the U.S. Senate, although it fell short of the 60 votes needed by Senate rules. Since 2007, at least 16 states have passed similar five-month abortion prohibitions. These laws are necessary to protect both unborn children and women themselves from dangerous late-term abortions. Peer-reviewed medical studies document the risk to women's mental and physical health from late-term abortions. A clear legal limit (instead of the Court's vague viability rule) is needed to mitigate this danger, and is supported by nearly everyone but Planned Parenthood.

NO TAXPAYER FUNDING OF ABORTION

Millions of Americans are opposed to the use of their tax dollars to pay for abortion. The Hyde amendment — which many wrongly think prevents all federal funding of abortion — does not apply to the Affordable Care Act, or comprehensively across the federal government, and is an annual rider rather than a permanent law.

The next president should sign the No Taxpayer Funding of Abortion Act, which would establish a government-wide statutory prohibition on abortion funding. This approach would reduce the need for numerous separate abortion-funding policies and ensure that no program or agency is exempt from this important safeguard, making the Hyde amendment comprehensive and permanent.

ENFORCEMENT OF FEDERAL CONSCIENCE-PROTECTION LAWS

Federal laws purport to protect the freedom to practice medicine without participating in abortion and the freedom not to pay for abortion or provide abortion coverage. Congresses and presidents of both parties have approved these conscience-protecting laws for decades. But the lack of appropriate redress for those who are robbed of these rights hamstrings the effectiveness of the laws that are supposed to protect them.

Nurses such as New York's Cathy DeCarlo should never be forced to participate in a late-term abortion. The clear harm DeCarlo suffered from forced abortion participation was only compounded when she had to wait for years for the HHS Office for Civil Rights to potentially take up her cause. The lack of consistent enforcement can discourage victims from pursuing vindication of their rights, and weaken incentives to follow the law. The ongoing failure of the HHS Office for Civil Rights to address California's illegal abortion-coverage mandate — a clear violation of the Weldon amendment — highlights the seriousness of the problem.

The next president should ensure timely enforcement of federal conscience-protection laws by HHS, and strengthen these laws by signing legislation, such as the Conscience Protection Act of 2016 (introduced in both the House and Senate), to provide a clear right for victims of illegal coercion to bring their own lawsuits. A private right of action more effectively deters coercion and, crucially, would ensure that protection of the fundamental right to provide care for patients without being required to participate in life-destroying and unethical activities does not hinge on the agenda of whoever occupies the White House.

REPEAL & REPLACE THE AFFORDABLE CARE ACT

Numerous anti-life and anti-conscience provisions are woven throughout the Affordable Care Act (ACA). For seven years, the Obama administration has vehemently pushed abortion-on-demand through its signature healthcare law, which compels citizens and employers to violate their consciences through subsidies of the procedure. The Health & Human Services (HHS) mandate, which forces employers to provide abortifacients (and contraceptives) through their employee health plans, is only the most prominent example of the ACA's radical anti-life intent.

The next president should support repeal of the ACA and promote, sign, and implement replacement bills that respect life: legislation that expressly prohibits funding for abortion and abortion coverage; that does not mandate coverage for other life-ending drugs and devices; that provides comprehensive conscience protections; that does not mandate or encourage the withholding, withdrawal, or curtailment of effective life-sustaining treatment to the elderly, terminally ill, chronically ill, disabled, or other vulnerable persons; and that does not place restrictions on the states' ability to enact and enforce legislation that protects and affirms life.

DISENTANGLE TAXPAYER-FUNDED PROGRAMS
FROM PLANNED PARENTHOOD

Since October, the House Select Committee on Infant Lives has been investigating Planned Parenthood's harvesting, trafficking, and sale of tissue from aborted children. By January, the committee should issue its report on these practices, including whether they violate five separate federal laws or whether the laws need to be amended to effectively punish the unethical practices they were intended to prevent.

But trafficking infant body parts is not the first and only scandal that should disqualify Planned Parenthood from receiving taxpayer dollars. Audit reports and whistleblower lawsuits from across the country have documented a pattern of abuse of taxpayer-funded programs by Planned Parenthood affiliates.

In a time of a massive federal deficits that threaten the future economic security of every American, the largest abortion provider in country, Planned Parenthood, should not be receiving 538 million tax dollars from federal and joint federal-state programs. Those taxpayer dollars would be better spent on community health centers or state and local health departments that can provide comprehensive care.

In addition to signing the No Taxpayer Funding for Abortion Act, the next president should commit to ensuring a genuine separation of taxpayer dollars from the abortion industry. The Obama administration's Centers for Medicare and Medicaid Services (CMS) has repeatedly blocked states from disentangling their Medicaid programs from abortion providers. Relying on CMS's flawed interpretation of Medicaid's "free choice of provider provision," courts have held states hostage to funding the abortion industry with both federal and state taxpayer dollars. The next president should issue a correct interpretation of the Medicaid statute, allowing states to preserve the integrity of their Medicaid programs.

The next president should also direct HHS to issue new regulations for Title X, returning that federal funding stream to the rules that governed it during the Reagan era, which required that all funding recipients maintain a physical and accounting separation from all abortion, abortion-counseling, and abortion-referral activities. The Supreme Court's 1981 *Rust v. Sullivan* ruling determined that these regulations are constitutional and "amply justified."

The next president should also reinstate the Mexico City policy and enforce the Helms amendment, measures that ensure our tax dollars are not supporting and promoting abortion in other countries.

RESTORE HEALTH AND SAFETY REGULATIONS FOR ABORTION-INDUCING DRUGS

Abortion-inducing drugs pose serious health and safety concerns to women and girls by inducing a hemorrhage. This year, Obama's Food & Drug Administration (FDA) rescinded safety regulations governing the use of chemical abortions across the country. These changes extend the use of chemical abortion further into pregnancy (when it has greater complication rates), promote its unsupervised use at home, and rescind physician oversight, all of which increase its health risks for women.

This is one of many attempts by the Obama administration to undermine state abortion limits and expand the 1 million abortions performed in America each year. It should be reversed immediately by the next president to protect women from the significant risk of hemorrhage. The FDA's approval of RU-486 (Mifeprex®, mifepristone) should also be reconsidered, given that drug's known dangers to women.

ACCURATE DATA ON ABORTION AND ITS RISKS

The Supreme Court legalized abortion nationwide in 1973 without any adequate federal mechanism or agency to accurately and comprehensively track abortions, their complications, or deaths. The annual number of abortions recorded annually by the Centers for Disease Control (CDC) is merely an estimate. That public-health vacuum has continued for 43 years. Congress needs to pass, and the next president needs to sign, a national abortion-data-reporting law that comprehensively collects and reports abortion data. Many countries collect and report better data on abortion than the U.S. Without accurate data, women undergoing abortion cannot be fully informed of the procedure's risks, and thus cannot truly give informed consent.

THE BORN-ALIVE ABORTION SURVIVORS PROTECTION ACT

Congress passed the Born Alive Infants Protection Act (BAIPA) years ago, to ensure that every child who survives an abortion is protected by the law. But the bill was passed without effective enforcement mechanisms, and congressional hearings and other studies have found that it is not completely effective. New enforcement mechanisms and penalties need to be adopted by Congress and signed by the next president.

*   *   *

This list is not definitive. It offers just some of the policies that the next president should prioritize to protect human life. They are achievable, and they are supported by a majority of the American public. They represent the kind of pro-life agenda that should be prioritized from Day One in any administration. All that is required for them to become reality is a president committed to using his powers for the affirmation of a culture of life that respects both mothers and their unborn children.

This is not merely a domestic agenda; the U.S. president's influence in protecting human life is long-lasting and international in scope. The example that the U.S. sets domestically — and in our international priorities, including the kind of aid and assistance we choose to offer the world's most vulnerable people — has real, tangible consequences for those beyond our borders. Inspired by American tradition going back to the soaring words of the Declaration of Independence, guided by constitutional text, reinforced by American public opinion, and based on the public policy established by the states and federal law, the next president can establish a legacy of protecting the unique dignity of human life that will shape the 21st century and help to reverse negative trends across the world.

1. Can you identify any distortions of fact in this piece? If so, what?

2. The author argues for "accurate data on abortion and its risks," but fails to point out why the government cannot fund such research. How might the refusal to fund research weaken the anti-abortion position?

CHAPTER 5

WHAT THE MEDIA SAY

According to both sides, objectivity is in short supply when it comes to media coverage of abortion. This chapter will provide an overview of how abortion is depicted in the media from two broad angles. First, we will take a look at representations of women's reproductive health and abortion as depicted in popular culture. Since film is often a good barometer for pervasive mores and ideologies, two of the articles that follow deal with how the taboo subject of abortion has historically been filtered through the lens of Hollywood, and how these representations have changed over time. Secondly, we will examine the media's response to Katha Pollitt's influential 2014 book *Pro: Reclaiming Abortion Rights*.

America has always had a puritanical streak about sex, especially female sexuality. Owing to this, it is quite common in the movies to see female abortion seekers meeting an untimely demise at the hands of a negligent, unskilled, and illegal provider of illicit abortion. Films such as *If These Walls Could Talk* (1996) and *Revolutionary Road* (2008) depict this. It is possible, however, to view the ubiquitous botched abortion as social critique. It is difficult to view such tragic endings and not wonder whether safe, legal, affordable abortions, minus any accompanying social stigma, might have prevented these senseless deaths.

Moving back to the field of contemporary journalism, Kate Yoder takes issue with this view of the media's overly accepting and uncritical understanding of abortion as a social good, as argued by Katha Pollitt. Pollitt's book was widely praised for opening a cultural space in which abortion emerges as a responsible choice for many women, but those on the pro-life side resent a purportedly hegemonic media landscape that marginalizes their views.

"ILLEGAL ABORTIONS ONSCREEN: DEPICTIONS OF A PRE-'ROE' WORLD," BY GRETCHEN SISSION AND RENEE BRACEY SHERMAN, FROM *REWIRE*, JANUARY 21, 2016

HERE ARE SEVERAL FILMS WITH BREATHTAKING PERFORMANCES THAT PORTRAY ILLEGAL ABORTION, WHICH YOU CAN WATCH TO REFLECT ON HOW FAR WE'VE COME, OR ON HOW FAR WE STILL MUST GO IN THE FIGHT FOR ABORTION ACCESS.

January 22 marks 43 years since the Supreme Court ruled on *Roe v. Wade*, legalizing abortion in the United States. Prior to Roe, many people sought abortions from illegal providers, trained or untrained, who offered the service in secret.

In the generation since *Roe* was decided, some advocates have blamed young people's complacency around abortion on fleeting historical memory. While we actively, emphatically dispute these claims of complacency, we acknowledge that—for some people in our generation—the reality of illegal abortion is, and hopefully will always be, secondhand. This makes listening to real women's experiences with illegal abortion especially important.

It is in this context, and in honor of *Roe*, that we are providing several films with breathtaking performances that portray illegal abortion. While research has shown these abortion plotlines deviate from accuracy in important ways, we still recognize their potential to tell stories that allow the viewer to better understand, acknowledge, and remember the world before legal abortion. You can watch these films to reflect on how far we've come, or on how far we still must go in the fight for abortion access. (And yes, there are spoilers below!)

ALFIE (1966)

Michael Caine plays Alfie Elkins, a womanizing, mansplaining jerk who distastefully talks about the women he's shagging all over London directly to the audience. First, Alfie impregnates his girlfriend Gilda, whom he refuses to marry. (Gilda ends up raising the child without Alfie.) After a short stint in a rest home for a lung infection and mental health break, Alfie befriends Harry, a fellow patient, and later has a one-night stand with Harry's wife, Lily. To keep Harry from finding out, Alfie and Lily decide to schedule an abortion.

The abortion provider comes to Alfie's home to perform the abortion on a nervous Lily. Prior to beginning the abortion, the provider suspiciously questions the two about their relationship (to which Alfie claims no responsibility) and informs them that an abortion after 28 days is a crime, both legally and "against the unborn child." The provider induces the abortion and leaves Alfie to support Lily through the rest, which includes Alfie smacking her to stop her from crying during the pain. Alfie leaves Lily alone in the apartment to pass the pregnancy. Upon returning, Alfie sees the fetus and tears up, then runs to his downstairs neighbor's apartment to make sense of what he's experiencing.

"Come to think of it, I don't rightly know what I was expecting to see," he tells Murray Melvin, the neighbor. "Certainly not this perfectly formed being. I half-expected it to cry out. It didn't, of course. It couldn't have done. It could never have had any life in it. Not a proper life of its own. … And I thought to myself, You know what, Alfie? You know what you done? You murdered him." He seems to come to terms with their decision and decides to change some of his ways.

Alfie was released in 1966 and the depiction of abortion takes place in London, where abortion became legal the following year, prior to *Roe v. Wade*. Feeling a little icky after watching Michael Caine call women "birds" for 90 minutes? We suggest watching *The Cider House Rules* in which Caine redeems himself (see below!).

DIRTY DANCING (1987)

Dirty Dancing is probably the most famous and popular film with an abortion story, although most viewers seem to forget that an abortion is really what drives the entire plot of the film. At a summer resort, Frances "Baby" Houseman (Jennifer Grey) vacations with her family and crushes hard on the dance instructor Johnny Castle (Patrick Swayze). Johnny and his partner, Penny Johnson (Cynthia Rhodes), are scheduled to perform at another resort and risk losing their contract because Penny is pregnant and needs to be available for her abortion. In addition to the challenge of taking time off work, Penny is hard-pressed to find the money for it. Baby not only borrows money from her father, she volunteers to take Penny's place as Johnny's dance partner. After returning from their resort performance,

Baby and Johnny find an extremely ill Penny, who is terrified to go to the hospital and possibly be interrogated by the police. Baby runs to get her father, who is a doctor, and saves Penny's life. While you may have seen this film a thousand times, it highlights the need for paid sick leave, local abortion providers, and health insurance that covers abortion care, for all—all things we're still fighting for.

IF THESE WALLS COULD TALK (1996)

If These Walls Could Talk tells the story of three women in the same house, 22 years apart, all of whom are facing unexpected pregnancies: Claire (Demi Moore), Barbara (Sissy Spacek), and Christine (Anne Heche).

Claire is a widowed nurse in 1952, desperate to end a pregnancy that will shame her late husband's family. She keeps her pregnancy secret and receives only outright disdain when she discloses it to her sister-in-law. Claire tries to induce an abortion both with pills and knitting needles, but these efforts are unsuccessful. She avoids one illegal provider who seems too dangerous, and rules out another who is too expensive. Finally, she finds an illegal provider who comes to her home. He ignores her suggestions to wash his hands or sterilize his equipment, and in her desperation she has no way to make him take these basic safety measures. Claire later hemorrhages on her kitchen floor, and dies while calling for help.

Barbara is a housewife, student, and mother of four in 1974, who believes another child will disrupt both her and her daughter's educations. Though she later chooses to parent, Barbara is the only woman portrayed in the film as having support during her decision to possibly choose abortion.

In 1996, Christine is an architecture student who does not believe in abortion, but considers it anyway when she gets pregnant after an affair with her professor. Christine's roommate reminds her of her anti-choice beliefs and says she agrees with the angry mob of protesters outside the clinic. Moments after the completion of her abortion, Christine is seen cradling the head of her dying doctor (played by Cher), after she was shot by an anti-choice fanatic. The gruesomeness of Claire's illegal abortion is mirrored in the violence of the abortion provider's murder. Only Barbara's story, where she chooses to parent, is free of gore.

Two of the three women get an abortion, and both of those stories end with women dying on the floor. For the most part, these women are making their decisions alone, with little knowledge of their options, and viewers get the sense that they are tormented by the choice or trapped by any outcome. Indeed, none of the stories have happy endings: Claire dies, Barbara gives up her dreams, and Christine is traumatized. The movie adheres to the "safe, legal, and rare" mantra of the 1990s, with no sense that abortion can be valid, valuable, and stigma-free.

THE CIDER HOUSE RULES (1999)

The Cider House Rules thoughtfully depicts several situations in which women need abortions and the providers who offer them in 1943. The film is set at an orphanage in Maine, where women facing unintended pregnancies go to deliver their babies, who are raised there until they're adopted. Michael Caine won an Academy Award for his portrayal of Dr. Wilbur Larch, the obstetrician who runs the orphanage and illegally provides abortions.

Dr. Larch teaches Homer Wells (Tobey Maguire) about labor and delivery, as well as abortions, however Homer says he's morally opposed to providing them. "How can you not feel obligated to help them when they can't get help anywhere else?" Dr. Larch asks Homer. When a woman is found on the orphanage grounds, Dr. Larch takes her in and tries to save her life, but unfortunately she dies due to a punctured uterus by an untrained abortion provider. Dr. Larch forces Homer to look at the damage to her uterus, showing him the impact of refusing to offer care he is trained on. "If she had come to you four months ago and asked for a simple D and C [abortion procedure] what would you have done? Nothing!" he yells at Homer. "This is what doing nothing gets you. It means that somebody else is gonna do the job—some moron who doesn't know how."

While digging the woman's grave, the pair discuss Homer's reservations about abortion and the responsibility of doctors versus those seeking abortion care. After meeting Candy (Charlize Theron) and Wally (Paul Rudd), a couple seeking an abortion from Dr. Larch, Homer leaves the orphanage to explore the world and work on an apple orchard, where his refusal to perform abortions is tested by a young Black woman, Rose (Erykah Badu), who was raped and impregnated by her father, the orchard's field manager.

One of the most powerful scenes is between Candy and Rose, when Candy discloses that she had an abortion as an act of truth to tell Rose that she supports whatever decision she wants to make. Rose then discloses that she does not want to continue the pregnancy which was a result of incest. Homer has a change of heart, realizes his calling to become an obstetrician, and returns to perform the full spectrum of reproductive care at the orphanage.

VERA DRAKE (2004)

In post-World War II London, Vera (Imelda Staunton) is a kind house cleaner by day, and a compassionate illegal abortion provider by night. She has been providing abortions safely for 20 years, and views her work as helping young women. Vera does not accept payment for her work—although, unbeknownst to her, her partner does charge money for arranging the abortions. When one of Vera's patients nearly dies, she is arrested, tried, and sentenced to over two years in prison. In the last scene of the film, she meets other women incarcerated for performing abortions, and they share stories. In a parallel plot, the daughter of Vera's employer is raped and becomes pregnant; she is referred to a psychiatrist who coaches her through the process of accessing a legal, medically recommended abortion. This subplot highlights the gap between poor women, who are dependent on Vera's risky services, and women with resources, who can obtain safer, legally allowed procedures.

The film was publicly criticized by Jennifer Worth (whose memoir *Call the Midwife* was adapted into a television show, which itself features several stories of illegal abortion). Worth argued that the abortion method used in the film (flushing the uterus with soap and water) was extremely painful and often deadly—not the simple process shown on screen. This challenge is a good reminder that, even in the hands of a well-intentioned provider, illegal abortion carried a great risk. However, Worth also asserted that "abortionists were in it for the money." This claim is refuted by significant research, most notably Carole Joffe's *Doctors of Conscience*, which reveals that many doctors who provided illegal abortions were frequently motivated by concerns for their patients' health and well-being.

4 MONTHS, 3 WEEKS, AND 2 DAYS (2007) AVAILABLE ON HULU

This Romanian film follows the daylong saga of Otilia (Anamaria Marinca) supporting her friend Gabita (Laura Vasiliu), a 22-year-old college student, through an illegal abortion. On the recommendation of a friend, the women book a hotel room after scheduling an appointment with Mr. Bebe, an illegal provider. To ensure he will perform her abortion, Gabita lies and says she's two months along, but he realizes she's closer to five months, hence the film's title. Mr. Bebe is a misogynistic man who uses Gabita's plight to extort money and sex, and tells them that if anyone finds out, they would all serve time in jail for murder. He performs the abortion by inserting a tube into Gabita, tells her to lay down until the abortion is complete, then leaves. Otilia leaves the hotel for a few hours to celebrate her boyfriend's mother's birthday, where she discloses to her partner what she's been doing and they have a discussion about what they would do if she became pregnant. "You're ashamed to talk about it, but not do it?" she asks her boyfriend about using the pull-out method. When she returns to the hotel, she finds that Gabita's has passed the fetus and left it wrapped in a towel on the bathroom floor—in the film the fetus appears much older than 19 weeks.

While the film takes place more recently, it depicts what two friends must risk to obtain an illegal abortion.

REVOLUTIONARY ROAD (2008)

Revolutionary Road tells the story of April Wheeler (Kate Winslet) and her husband, Frank (Leonardo DiCaprio), who are living in the Connecticut suburbs in 1955. To their neighbors, they're the perfect couple, but in reality, they're trying to find their way back to the ecstatic relationship they had before their two children and ho-hum life. The couple is planning to leave their lives and move to Paris when April realizes she's pregnant again. "There are things we can do ... as long as we take care of it before 12 weeks it's fine," April tells Frank about her desire for an abortion. While Frank seems supportive of April at first, he becomes furious after finding the hidden instruments April was planning to use to induce her abortion. April tells Frank she's having an abortion for him (and because she doesn't want anymore children), but he tells her "the thought of it makes [his] stomach turn." The couple cancels their dream move to Paris to remain in their suburban life, which proves to be too much for April. The morning after a huge fight, April, acting normal, proceeds to self-induce her abortion while Frank is at work. In a tragic turn of events, April senses she is dying and calls an ambulance. She dies at the hospital.

The performances in this film are poignant and are sure to make you tear up. There's nothing more haunting than April's final scene during which she's bleeding out in her living room, which leaves the viewer questioning whether her death was due to suicide, her illegal abortion, or both.

While deaths like April's were recurrent during the pre-*Roe* era, deaths from abortion are extremely rare (less than 1 percent) today. Conversely, deaths from abortion are common in media depictions: Research found that over 15 percent of abortion plot lines show a woman's death after an abortion and of those almost 60 percent die from the procedure itself. This gives audiences the impression that abortion is unsafe and women having abortions are deserving of their imminent death.

FOR COLORED GIRLS (2010)

Unfortunately, the legalization of abortion did not mean that the promise of *Roe* would be reality for everyone. Policies like the Hyde Amendment and parental involvement laws make low-income people, women of color, and young people disproportionately unable to access safe abortion care and can be forced to seek out untrained providers.

In *For Colored Girls*, Nyla/Purple (Tessa Thompson) is a 16-year-old dancer who just graduated high school and describes her excitement of having sex for the first time after graduation. Nyla realizes she's pregnant and goes to her sister Tangie (Thandie Newton) for "college application money," but it's really for an abortion. "I remember the first time I got pregnant, I was so scared," Tangie recalls and proceeds to tell her about an apartment she went to, and afterwards she "wasn't pregnant anymore." Out of jealousy, Tangie refuses to give Nyla any money and Nyla is left with no choice but to go to a literal back-alley apartment for an abortion. A negligee-clad woman (Macy Gray) drinks alcohol and smokes cigarettes while using dirty tools from a bucket to perform Nyla's abortion.

After passing out in the street, Nyla is rushed to the hospital where she poetically recounts the grimy scene of her abortion to her overbearing mother, Alice (Whoopi Goldberg), and a social worker (Kerry Washington). Upon hearing the story, Alice argues with Tangie about her previous abortion, which Tangie admits she didn't want but was forced to have by Alice. During an emotional scene, both women come clean about their experiences of incest at the hand of their father/grandfather.

For Colored Girls is a tragic account of several Black women's experiences with rape, abuse in many forms, suicide, various reproductive issues, and homophobic HIV-stigma. It carries many trigger warnings.

1. Which of these films seems most progressive about abortion? Likewise, which films seem to most explicitly "punish" women who choose abortion?

2. Do you think film representations of abortion are inherently political in content, or do you think they are there simply to advance the plot or create drama? Does this vary from film to film?

"GRANDMA'S MATRILINEAL ROAD TRIP: A CONVERSATION ACROSS GENERATIONS," BY RUTH RIDDICK, FROM *CONSCIENCE*, A TRADEMARK OF CATHOLICS FOR CHOICE, SPRING 2016

"WHERE CAN YOU GET A REASONABLY PRICED ABORTION IN THIS TOWN?" --ELLE REID (LILY TOMLIN), *GRANDMA*

"My favorite part of *Grandma* was the way in which it treated Sage's abortion as a logical, conscientious decision," says social justice advocate Meghan Smith, recent nominee for the win Young Women of Achievement award. "I'm so accustomed to the media portraying abortion as a difficult decision and treating abortion as a punishment or consequence for other things."

When was the last time you saw the abortion experience normalized in movies? At the local multiplex? Better yet, when was the last time you saw multigenerational mainstream movie stars organize an abortion for one of their own? And in a comedy? "It was alternately poignant and funny as hell," is Catholics for Choice board member Janet Gallagher's verdict. "I loved the realistic portrayal of family tensions and mutual incomprehension among women of such different generations."

The setup in *Grandma* is straightforward: Sage (Julia Garner) is a young woman who wants an abortion but doesn't have the money. Preferring not to involve her mother, Judy (Marcia Gay Harden), she appeals to her take-charge grandmother Elle (Lily Tomlin), a supporter of legalization from the pre-*Roe* era. Timing is not Sage's strong suit here: In a device to set the story in motion, Elle has just cut up her credit cards, making a whimsical mobile of the pieces. These two must set out to find the necessary funds. The movie is a chronicle of their road trip.

Even though it isn't a plot point, Smith was immediately aware of the limitations of that very road trip, and she's not talking about the deplorable state of Elle's vehicle. "In Massachusetts, where I live, minors need parental consent or a judicial bypass in order to access abortion care, and so Sage's journey would have been even harder here," she says. "And I was reminded of anti-choice proposals that have popped up several times at the federal level, which would have prevented Elle from being able to help Sage if they had crossed state lines."

For activists of Elle's generation, this increasingly limited access to legal abortion is unthinkable. Janet Gallagher observes, "The segment I found most moving was the Lily Tomlin character driving to a building she assumes will still house a women's health center providing abortion at a lower cost. When they get there, the center has been replaced by a cafe serving pretentious coffee. ... The clinic has been gentrified out." (Elle responds by throwing a fit at the coffee shop—hilarious if it weren't so impotent.)

"What struck me was the difficulty of sustaining the alternative, communal and nonprofit resources we created in the 1960s and 70s—clinics, bookstores, food co-ops—that allowed many of us to pour time and energy into the movements of that era," Gallagher says. Before our eyes, Elle gets a comprehensive education in just how unsustainable these resources have proved.

Unlike Elle, Gallagher came to the prochoice cause reluctantly. "As a Catholic just recently out of the novitiate, I was conflicted about abortion," she explains. "Discussion in my consciousness-raising group led me to realize that my Quaker/pacifist sisters felt very differently."

Gallagher became involved in reproductive rights specifically to support access to legal abortion. "When the Hyde Amendment cut off Medicaid funding for abortion in 1976, my social justice values and respect for the consciences of other women led me into activism," she recalls.

Decades later, women face the same issues. "I kept thinking about the clients with whom I work on the hotline for my local abortion fund," says Meghan Smith. "Sage's struggle to find enough cash to cover her abortion therefore rang very true to me. I was also reminded of friends in high school who had to travel across the state line to get to the closest Planned Parenthood for basic well-woman visits but who paid in cash because they were afraid of their parents finding out. Or who tried to buy birth control pills from friends because they couldn't get to a clinic or didn't want it showing up on insurance."

"Meghan and other younger activists' work on setting up local abortion funds seems a new version of that direct-service model offered by volunteers at the Women's Health & Abortion Project in the early 1970s," Gallagher adds. "Once New York legalized (about three years pre-*Roe*), women from all over the country headed here in desperation. Volunteers would pick them up at the airport and arrange places for them to stay. I remember out-of-towners in sleeping bags on the living room floor of a Brooklyn commune. It was like a different kind of underground railway."

The more things change, the more they stay the same.

And where is the unsuspecting Judy while her mother and daughter take to the road in Elle's rickety car? At the office, putting in the long, family-unfriendly hours mandatory for maintaining a contemporary working life. Judy belongs to the generation for whom the choice of having both career and children was the liberating promise of the second wave's reproductive rights struggle. We didn't anticipate that rights hard won need harder defense. Indeed, in the heady days of expanding options, we presumed that the abortion issue was settled and we could move on.

In truth, women in Judy's position are exhausted to the bone by the double-shift demands of work and home.

Janet Gallagher is acutely aware of the stakes: "Perhaps Judy's frenetic pursuit of her career represents a reaction against the economic insecurity embodied by her mother," she suggests. "Elle's economic situation, her inability to give her granddaughter the money she needs for an abortion, reflect the costs paid now by aging activists for the assumption that we would transform reality and not need to concentrate on individual economic security."

"I was ready for the film to treat Sage's abortion as a [negative] consequence of Judy's focus on her career," says Meghan Smith. Introduced late in the film, Judy is set up for judgment as a villain. It doesn't happen. As Smith notes, "The sweetness of Judy's appearance at the clinic, her support in the end, the way in which Sage's abortion actually brought the family closer together. ... These all seemed more realistic and complicated and important than the tired 'abortion as a punishment' tropes that I've seen in other media portrayals."

Are there any men in *Grandma*? Fittingly, Sage's boyfriend puts in an appearance: a loser-in-training—where do we find these creatures? And why? He's no more prepared for parenthood than she is. Neither, alas, is he prepared to take any responsibility, which affords Elle an opportunity to put him straight in a few (wish-fulfilling?) moves. "Meeting Sage's boyfriend was only affirmation of the appropriateness of Sage's decision," Smith notes approvingly. "Not a mechanism to shame her for having sex in the first place."

And, famously, there's Sam Elliott's cameo. The saddest chapter of this odyssey is a conscience-searing rebuke to those of us who, back in the day and irrespective of whether we shared children, excoriated the men who tried to be in our lives for the systemic sins of the patriarchy. (Every revolution has its victims?) Elliott's character, angry still, remarks to Elle, "I thought you came to offer amends." To the movie's credit, this leftover business is not resolved.

What next?

Sage has her abortion with the support of both mother and grandmother. A truce is established between the generations. "The moment when Sage realizes that her mother, in fact, wants to help—and has had her own struggles—is a beautiful depiction of the ways in which women my age can sometimes forget that our mothers had to navigate careers, families and policies and climates that weren't necessarily friendly," says Smith.

Elle is perhaps a little less alone than when we met at the start of this eventful day, for all that she's shown on her own in the film's final images. All three have earned our respect and affection. It's the happy ending that's available, and we are invited to agree that it's enough for now.

But, for us, there's more to the story: "The Elle generation has to rejoin the political, legislative battle for abortion access and funding," says Janet Gallagher. "We also need to join our younger sisters in organizing and funding local abortion funds that will serve low-income women."

From her perspective as a Millennial, Meghan Smith agrees, "I thought of *Grandma* as portraying two important challenges facing my generation: the challenge of abortion access and the challenge of relating to, and learning from, our mothers' and grandmothers' generations."

"When Sage asks her grandmother for financial help, we could look at it as simply a fact of the current state of abortion access for young women," she concludes. "That the film mostly seems to stick to this view is a sad, but to me, accurate commentary on the political battles that my generation will have to fight—and is fighting." Forty years later. Just ask "Grandma."

1. Based on this description, do you think *Grandma* depicts the young woman seeking an abortion in a more positive light than most films?

2. What lessons regarding economic class, generational conflict, and political activism emerge from this reading of the film?

"LIES IN THE EXAM ROOM," FROM *WOMEN'S HEALTH ACTIVIST*, A NEWSLETTER FOR THE NATIONAL WOMEN'S HEALTH NETWORK, SEPTEMBER 9, 2016

Opponents of reproductive choice have spent years attempting to frighten women by spreading misinformation about a non-existent link between having an abortion and an increased risk of breast cancer. There is no evidence of such a link, and no research scientists or breast cancer activists support the claim. Nonetheless, anti-choice organizations continue their attempts to disseminate this myth through advertising campaigns and so-called "informed consent laws."

The faulty arguments used to promote the non-existent link between abortion and breast cancer are based on selected "case studies." These studies have crucial methodological flaws that complicate the supposed abortion/cancer link. Many of these flawed studies asked women to report their abortion history retrospectively, often many years after the abortion procedure. This sort of retrospective data-gathering can lead to reporting bias (or "recall bias") that confuse data and analysis. Further, women who have been diagnosed with breast cancer are more likely to report having had an abortion, because they are identifying their early risk factors and are likely to recall ones that have received media attention, like abortion or oral contraceptive use.[1]

As a result of these methodological flaws in the case studies, the relationship between abortion and breast cancer seems greater than it actually is.

In contrast to case studies, more accurate information is obtained from "prospective cohort studies." In these investigations, researchers start tracking study participants at a certain time and follow them for many years to get information about a specific question: in this case, which women are likely to develop breast cancer later in life. The format of these studies means that participants are much less likely to suffer from recall and reporting biases.

None of the prospective cohort studies have found a significant association between breast cancer and having had an abortion. A table summarizing the results of rigorous cohort studies is available at: https://ww5.komen.org/BreastCancer/Tab/e25Abortionandbreastcancerrisk.html.[2]

In early 2014, a meta-analysis from China that seemed to find a relationship between breast cancer and abortion received a lot of attention from anti-abortion activists.[3] The study, however, was filled with methodological flaws that severely limit its validity. Specifically, the analysis reviewed 36 previous Chinese studies, only eight of which had well-designed methodologies. And, none of these eight well-conducted studies showed a significant relationship between breast cancer and abortion. Many of the other poorly designed studies were not published in peer-reviewed journals, which is the scientific gold-standard for reliable evidence. The study also included contradictory findings about whether abortion-related stigma played a role in women's reporting of having had the procedure.

RESEARCH FINDINGS

Since 2003, the National Cancer Institute (NCI) and the American College of Obstetricians and Gynecologists (ACOG) have reviewed the evidence on abortion and cancer and assessed the research. These leading medical experts have consistently and unanimously agreed that the evidence is strong that *having an abortion does not increase a woman's risk of breast cancer.*

As a result of the NCI and ACOG review of available evidence, the organizations declared that recent studies demonstrated no "causal relationship between induced abortion and a subsequent increase in breast cancer risk." The organizations re-examined the evidence again and reaffirmed this statement in 2009 and 2013.[4]

Studies with robust methodological designs repeatedly find no indication that having an abortion increases a woman's risk of breast cancer. For example:

- One of the strongest studies on abortion and breast cancer, a 1997 Danish study published in *The New England Journal of Medicine*, reported on the experience of over 300,000 women who had had abortions.[5] It found that those women were no more likely to develop breast cancer than were the 1.2 million women with no history of abortion.
- A large prospective study reported on by Harvard researchers in 2007 included more than 100,000 women and found no connection to breast cancer for either spontaneous or induced abortions.[6] Women were tracked between 1993 and 2003. Since they were asked about abortion at the start of the study, recall bias was unlikely to play a role in the findings.

- In 2008, the California Teachers Study reported on 100,000 women who had been followed since 1995. The participants were asked about past induced and spontaneous abortions at the start of the study in 1995.[7] More than 3,300 participants developed breast cancer; there was no difference in cancer risk between women who had had an abortion and those who had not.
- The Collaborative Group on Hormonal Factors in Breast Cancer conducted a large and expansive meta-analysis of 53 studies in 16 countries that included 83,000 women in 2004; it concluded that "the totality of worldwide epidemiological evidence indicates that pregnancies ending as either spontaneous or induced abortions do not have adverse effects on women's subsequent risk of developing breast cancer."[8]

The bottom line is: there is currently no scientifically-based evidence that abortion leads to an increased risk of breast cancer.

COUNTERING THE ANTI-CHOICE SCARE TACTICS

Anti-choice organizations have long used this supposed correlation between abortion and breast cancer to incite fear and promote their anti-abortion agenda. Back in 1996, the anti-choice group Christ's Bride Ministries published misleading ads in the transit systems of several cities including Washington, D.C., Baltimore, Philadelphia, and Chicago. These ads stated that "women who choose abortion suffer more and deadlier breast cancer."

The public health, reproductive rights, and breast cancer advocacy communities responded quickly. Dr. Philip Lee, Assistant Secretary of Health in the U.S. Department of Health and Human Services, wrote a letter stating that the ad is "unfortunately misleading, unduly alarming, and does not accurately reflect the weight of the scientific literature." The National Cancer Institute issued a fact sheet asserting that the statements "misrepresent the information in the scientific literature."[9] And the National Breast Cancer Coalition published a position paper pointing out that "the abortion rate has been fairly constant since 1978, while breast cancer incidence continues to rise."[10]

Despite the outcry from the public health community, anti-choice activists are using misinformation as a way to scare women out of having an abortion. Many states have considered and/or passed legislation forcing clinicians to provide women with false information about the effects of abortion, including the purported connection with breast cancer.

Currently, 17 states mandate that women seeking abortion care be given "counseling" that includes specific misinformation.[11] Five states (Alaska, Kansas, Mississippi, Oklahoma, Texas) mandate that women seeking abortion care receive medically inaccurate information that abortion leads to breast cancer.[12,13] North Dakota requires that its abortion counseling materials discuss "the possible increased risk of breast cancer."[14] (Twelve states mandate that women be given misinformation about the fetus' ability to feel pain, and seven states mandate provision of medically inaccurate information on abortion's long-term mental health effects.[15,16])

Breast cancer and reproductive rights activists are working to prevent the passage of laws requiring women to hear medically inaccurate information and to ensure that women get sound medical advice when considering abortion care. The NWHN is committed to ensuring that women have access to accurate, balanced information about the all reproductive services, including abortion. Keep an eye out for scare tactics in your community, and let us know what you find.

1. Do you think data that links abortion to breast cancer has any possible validity?

2. If you answered no above, do you think this is a way to discourage abortion "by any means necessary"? Might the deliberate spreading of misinformation backfire?

"TOP 10 WAYS MEDIA SPIN ABORTION AS 'MORAL,' 'SOCIAL GOOD'," BY KATIE YODER, FROM *NEWSBUSTERS*, OCTOBER 2014

A new book – a gospel of responsibility-free sex – defines abortion as "right," "good" and "moral." It's what's "best for kids" and it's all about a woman's "unalienable right" to pursue happiness. When Katha Pollitt, an outspoken feminist and columnist for The Nation, published "Pro:

Reclaiming Abortion Rights" on Oct. 14, the journalists used it as a launching pad for their latest abortion obsession: no-fault abortion. Pollitt's book "reframes abortion" as "a moral right with positive social implications." And since nobody ever went broke telling the self-obsessed what they want to hear, the book has received rapturous praise form the feminist left.

Here, as given to us by Pollitt's media acolytes, are the tenets of the new Church of Guilt-Free Abortion.

1. SLATE: ABORTION IS 'GREAT,' A 'POSITIVE SOCIAL GOOD'

"Abortion Is Great," began Slate's Hanna Rosin in her book review. She reasoned, "As Pollitt puts it, 'This is not the right time for me' should be reason enough." "Saying that aloud," she said, "would help push back against the lingering notion that it's unnatural for a woman to choose herself over others."

Trashing the pro-life movement, Rosin again cited Pollitt to argue, "we have all essentially been brainwashed by a small minority of prolife activists" – or the "loud minority [that] has beaten the rest of us into submission with their fetus posters and their absolutism and their infiltration of American politics" instead of "saying out loud that abortion is a positive social good."

As far as messaging, "The pro-choice side should be able to say that a poor or working-class woman getting an abortion is making a wise choice for her future," Rosin wrote, "That way, the left would own not only gender and income equality, but also a new era of family values."

2. REFINERY 29: ABORTION IS A 'SOCIAL GOOD' FOR WOMEN TO 'LIVE FULL, COMPLETE LIVES'

Like Rosin, Refinery 29's Sarah Jaffe urged, "It is past time for a revived, unapologetic and unified abortion rights movement that understands abortion as a social good."

Jaffe celebrated the book's "powerful call to understand abortion not as some singular culture-war issue but as one part of a struggle for women to be able to live full, complete lives."

Change, she said, "will come from many more people joining a revitalized movement that is able, as Pollitt argues, to stop conceding territory and, yes, demand abortion be part of any true struggle for social justice."

3. THE GUARDIAN: ABORTION IS 'WOMEN'S PURSUIT OF HAPPINESS AS AN UNALIENABLE RIGHT'

"Abortion isn't about the right to privacy. It's about women's right to equality," began Jessica Valenti for The Guardian. But "The hard part about arguing that abortion is necessary for women's equality, of course, is that there are still too many people who don't see women's pursuit of happiness as an unalienable right," she whined.

Not one to play around, Valenti quickly went to the crux of her argument: "It's time for the pro-choice movement to lose the protective talking points and stop dancing around the bigger truth: Abortion is good for women."

She explained:

"The pro-choice movement needs to put the opposition on its heels, and make what some in the 'pro-forced birth ' movement say what they're really thinking: that it's more important for women be mothers than go to college; that the ability to support existing children, to have a job that pays well or to pursue a career path we love are inconsequential realities compared to embracing our 'natural ' role as perpetually pregnant; that a woman's ability to incubate a fetus trumps any other contribution to society that she could possibly make."

4. BUSTLE: ABORTION IS 'THE BEST FOR KIDS'

Bustle's Lisa Levy praised Pollitt's "elegant, pointed, and smart" book as an "explanation of why keeping abortion legal is so critical to women's lives." In her piece, she listed the "7 Things I Learned from Coffee with Katha" – such as "Keeping abortion legal is not only the best situation for women – it's the best for kids, too."

"Abortion is a crucial way to make sure all babies are wanted, and their mothers are able to nurture and provide for them and help them to realize their potential," Levy worshipped.

5. THE HUFFINGTON POST: ABORTION IS 'MORE MORAL' THAN HAVING A CHILD, PART OF MOTHERHOOD

To announce Pollitt's book, The Huffington Post published an excerpt where Pollitt recognized abortion as "part of the fabric of American life." "We need to see abortion as an urgent practical decision that is just as moral as the decision to have a child – indeed, sometimes more moral," Pollitt spurted.

"Actually," she continued, "abortion is part of being a mother and of caring for children, because part of caring for children is knowing when it's not a good idea to bring them into the world."

HuffPo later invited Katha Pollitt on for an interview on HuffPost Live.

6. THE WASHINGTON POST: ABORTION IS WORTHY OF 'POP CULTURE'

Alyssa Rosenberg reviewed the Pollitt's book with a different twist: "Why it is so important that pop culture be able to discuss abortion."

The book, she wrote, "reaffirmed my longstanding conviction that it is important for pop culture to get more confident and less coy in talking about abortion."

In her conclusion, she decided, "If Hollywood really wanted to show off its ability to shape public consciousness and change the conversation in the same way it contributed to the gay rights movement, 'Pro' ought to be a challenge to that industry to prove it can do what politicians cannot."

7. ELLE: ABORTION IS ENDING 'POTENTIAL LIFE, NOT A LIFE-LIFE'

Elle's Laurie Abraham not only interviewed Pollitt, but read her book as a "kind of call to action, an appeal to stop letting abortion opponents fill all the available airspace." Or, in other words, a call to "tell a different story, the more common yet strangely hidden one, which is that I don't feel guilty and tortured about my abortion. Or rather, my abortions."

She did so for Elle's November 2014 issue in a piece entitled, "Abortion: Not Easy, Not Sorry."

As a "highly educated daughter of a Planned Parenthood clinic volunteer," Abraham believed, "An embryo or a fetus is all potential." "Now is the time to say that I don't think that I killed anyone when I had an abortion," she said.

To describe her first abortion, Pollitt wrote:

"By 12 weeks, it has become a fetus, 2 inches to 3 inches long, with features that are recognizably human. Yet by my lights, a fetus at this stage is not a person in any real sense of that word. It can't live outside the womb; none of its organ systems is fully developed; and, most crucially, it's not capable of conscious thought, since the cortical synapses don't begin to form until the second trimester. The way I've always thought of it, in lay terms, is that I ended a potential life, not a life-life."

While "she sobbed" before her second abortion, she reasoned, "A third child would put too much strain on our marriage, I wanted to keep working, and I didn't want to cheat the children I already had."

8. THE NEW YORK TIMES: ABORTION IS A 'RIGHT'

For The New York Times, Clara Jeffery recognized the book as an "eye opener for those who have never darkened the door of a women's studies classroom."

Although she never had an abortion herself, she helped friends terminate their unborn. Jeffery noted how, "contraception and abortion have allowed women to widen their worlds dramatically."

"If you're a woman, I don't need to detail all the barriers we still face," she assumed. "If you're a mother, I don't need to tell you all the ways in which the workplace is set up as if you didn't have kids, and schools, camps and childhood extracurriculars as if you didn't have a job."

"Motherhood is hard enough if you go into it willingly," she said. "And Pollitt is correct to insist that the right to an abortion is merely society's down payment on all the rights we are yet due."

9. NEW YORK MAGAZINE: ABORTION IS 'GOOD FOR EVERYONE'

"We should accept that it's good for everyone if women have only the children they want and can raise well," Alex Ronan wrote for The Cut, "which is both obvious and worth repeating in a climate that's openly hostile to women's lives, safety, and ambitions."

And Pollitt was the best champion of the cause. "Blending statistics, history, and stories of real women along with her signature wit, Pollitt is an excellent guide to the debate's most important questions," Ronan continued.

10. SALON: ABORTION IS VALUING WOMEN

Salon's Michele Filgate described Pollitt's book as "a refreshing and comprehensive look at abortion rights." Because, as Filgate whined, "There are many preconceived notions about abortion that lead to one terrible conclusion: our society doesn't value women nearly enough."

"One would think that in 2014, all women in the United States would have easy access, but that's somehow not the case," she said. "'Pro' is a passionate plea – and a book that is needed now more than ever."

11 …

That is the media take. That is the "feminist" take: the voices of women who regret their abortions, pro-life women, baby girls who are no more, don't exist.

Let's prove them wrong.

1. The author identifies several recent arguments that reframe abortion as socially positive. Do these views align with your own?

2. Do you think abortion is an essentially private matter that should not be "spun" one way or the other? Or is each individual decision inherently political? Explain your view.

CHAPTER 6

WHAT ORDINARY PEOPLE SAY

While Americans are highly opinionated about abortion, recent polling suggests that the wide majority nonetheless favor flexible, "non-absolutist" positions. In other words, only a small minority feels that abortion should always be legal, at any stage of a woman's pregnancy. Likewise, just a small minority think abortion should be illegal across the board. This suggests there is much common ground in the abortion debate—a counterintuitive, if encouraging sign. Predictably, opinions on abortion map neatly to other facets of self-identification such as religious background or political affiliation. For example, according to a Pew Research study, 60 percent of Republicans oppose abortion rights, a percentage that increases as we move to the right wing extremes of the party. Such non-absolutist views on abortion are fairly consistent across race, education, and sex. This has been the case since 1995.

Despite the fact that the majority of Americans support the constitutionally protected right to a safe and legal abortion in most cases, pushback against abortion rights continues unabated on the state level. This is occurring while Americans simultaneously embrace increasingly progressive positions on social issues such as same sex marriage, immigration, and economic policy, for example. Such dissonance begs explanation.

Statistics and broad overviews provide an accurate picture of societal attitudes toward abortion, but to really understand the complex and often contradictory attitudes ordinary people hold on the subject, it is necessary to zoom in on the lived experience of individual women. In this chapter, we will hear from Laura Stradiotto, a thirty-something Canadian mother of two, who with the full support of her husband chose to terminate an unplanned pregnancy. Her story, though seldom told, is not unusual. In sharing her experience, Stradiotto redresses stereotypes that only irresponsible teens have abortions. In fact, the author had to reexamine her own judgmental attitudes toward younger women while going through the abortion process.

"NOT THE RIGHT TIME," BY LAURA STRADIOTTO, FROM *CHATELAINE*, SEPTEMBER 2016

I was happily married with two small kids. Then I found out I was pregnant. I had an abortion—a decision more women in their 30s and 40s are making than ever before. So why aren't we talking about it?

Driving through the Rockies, heading to a friend's wedding, back in 2010, I tried to hold down my lunch. I imagined it was the altitude or car sickness, but by the time we stopped for the night in Canmore, Alta., all I wanted to do was lie down. I felt queasy. I couldn't finish my glass of wine at dinner. I put my two-year-old son and six-month-old daughter to bed, curled up beside them and was out for the night.

As our family vacation neared its end, I felt no better than when we'd left our home in Northern Ontario one week before. My stomach was bloated, my head clouded like I was hungover. On the journey back, a little voice in the back of my head was getting louder and louder: Take a pregnancy test.

But how could I be pregnant? Since the birth of our second six months earlier, I could count on one hand the number of times my husband and I had had sex. With breastfeeding, night waking and the start of my son's terrible-twos tantrums, I wasn't in the mood. Still, I drove to the closest pharmacy and picked up a pregnancy test. I've peed on these sticks before, but I didn't feel the same adrenaline rush I had in the past. Just dread. When the pink line appeared across the window, my legs weakened and my skin flushed. I felt powerless, like someone had pinned me down.

I opened the bathroom door. My husband was sorting through a pile of dirty laundry. "I'm pregnant," I said. We sat down at the kitchen table with two glasses of red wine. My husband was working 70-hour weeks in the restaurant industry, and I was the primary caregiver to our children. My son still woke up crying several times a night, and I was nursing my daughter every few hours. Both wanted only me for comfort. I loved my babies to bits, but I was emotionally and physically drained.

I was also on two back-to-back maternity leaves, with no EI for the current one because I hadn't gone back to work after the first. I had even been debating whether to resign from my job as a reporter to work part-time or from home. We were not opposed to having more children, and there was a tiny part of me that thought we could make this work. Maybe if I had some help. Maybe if the kids were in daycare.

But the reality was we couldn't afford child care for two kids, and my husband couldn't cut back his hours at work. Our own parents were still working full-time, too, and I knew the responsibility of caring for all three kids would fall on me. I understood my capabilities and limitations as a mother. I would never be able to handle three children under three years old. It would place insurmountable pressure on my family, and I worried it would end my marriage. That night, we decided, together, to terminate the pregnancy.

I was raised a Roman Catholic, and so was my husband. We were told that abortion is a sin, just as wrong as adultery and murder. I'm not sure when I deviated from my religious upbringing, but I always believed a woman should be able to make her own decisions regarding reproductive health. At my all-girls Catholic high school, during a discussion on abortion, I was the only student in the class who said I'd terminate a pregnancy if my life were at risk. Everyone else said they couldn't imagine killing their unborn baby. My rationale was based on logic: Was my life not valuable? What if I had other children to take care of? So when I faced an unplanned pregnancy, I did not pray to God for guidance. Instead, my husband and I trusted each other.

Within a few days, I made an appointment at a local hospital's "options clinic" and spoke to the nurse, who explained my choices. But I had come in knowing what I wanted. After an ultrasound revealed I was seven or eight weeks pregnant, I had to wait another week for the procedure. It was the longest week of my life. I wanted it to be over.

When I finally found myself in the hospital waiting room, I was asked to sit in a corner designated for patients undergoing the same procedure, which allowed the doctor who would perform the abortions to address everyone at once. There were seven of us.

Sitting under the bright fluorescent lighting early that Friday morning, we were strangers with a common secret. But eavesdropping on these young women chit-chatting about boyfriends and social lives, I convinced myself that I was different. I was the oldest one there by a good five or 10 years. I wasn't single and promiscuous. I was a 32-year-old mother of two with responsibilities. I knew it was wrong to judge, but I found myself doing just that. The procedure seemed routine to them. One young woman revealed it wasn't her first abortion. Another teen, accompanied by her mother, spoke openly about her decision: She was in high school and couldn't manage a baby. The other women nodded in agreement.

I wanted to escape that corner of the room. I searched for something familiar and picked up an Archie comic. Glancing up periodically from its pages, I recognized many of the nurses and doctors in the hospital. They dined in the same restaurants and shopped at the same grocery stores as my husband and me. They lived in my neighbourhood. One nurse walked up to me and asked how I was. I didn't know what to say. She must have known why I was there.

I was home before noon, feeling groggy and cramped, and as soon as my head hit the pillow, I was out. My husband spent the afternoon with the kids and let me sleep for a few hours. Convincing him I was okay—or forcing myself to resume a routine—I took over and he went back to work. That evening, a friend came over with her toddler and we watched the kids chase each other around the living room while I held my youngest. I don't think I even offered her anything to drink. She was trying to have another baby and had suffered several miscarriages. I didn't dare tell her about my day.

My husband and I barely spoke about the abortion. And I was okay with that. I wanted to forget and I thought not talking about it would help me move forward. The truth was, for weeks after, I thought about the abortion constantly. I remembered the miraculous feeling of a tiny life growing inside of me. I would estimate how far along the fetus would be. For strength, I reminded myself why I'd had the abortion in the first place: to be a better mother. It became a mantra.

I resigned from my full-time job and started to freelance from home. I said it would help balance my family and work life. But I made this career move largely to honour my reason for ending the pregnancy. As my son and daughter became little independent human beings, my husband and our extended family stepped in to play a larger role in their lives. My children no longer depended on me every waking—and sleeping—moment, and they were thriving. It was a huge relief. I felt closer to my husband than ever before. I was more relaxed as a mom and could dedicate more time to my career. Our family was in a good financial position. So when I learned in early 2013 that I was expecting, there was no sense of doom. It was different this time around. We welcomed our third child, a boy, in late 2013.

Over the years, I've started to open up to some friends and family about having an abortion. Three years ago, my sister, a young mother of two who has suffered from severe postpartum depression, learned she was pregnant. The father didn't want another child. She did, but she was traumatized by her previous depression and afraid the same sense of paralysis would return. I wanted to let her know that she had options. Most important, I wanted her to know I supported her unconditionally. Accompanied by her partner, she made the trip to a Toronto clinic a few days later.

Then, last summer, I was sitting with a friend in a coffee shop, reading the paper, when I saw that Health Canada had approved mifepristone, a pill used at home to end pregnancy in the first trimester. The article debated the drug's legal and moral implications and said that many pro-life organizations wanted the government to stop distribution. That stance felt like a personal attack. If this drug had been available to me six years ago, I would have, without a doubt, used it and spared myself the humiliation of having to go to a hospital in a small town. "I had an abortion," I blurted out to my friend as I read the news. It was the first time I'd said it without hesitation or fear. She was taken aback but acknowledged the decision must have been a tough one. "I don't regret it," I said. "It was the best decision I could've made for my family." We sat in silence for a while and then I turned the page to the arts section.

That coffee shop conversation stayed with me. I realized that not only was I okay with having had an abortion, I wanted to share my experience and defend my decision. I had been stunned to learn that one out of every three Canadian women under the age of 45 has had an abortion. If abortion is this common, why aren't women talking about it more openly? What is preventing more of us from taking a stand on the right to access abortion services and assert control over our reproductive choices? Six years ago, sitting in that hospital waiting room, I was convinced I didn't belong with the other women there. I identified as pro-choice, but I harboured my own stereotypes: Women who had abortions were young and irresponsible, not wives and mothers like me. In fact, in 2011, there were more abortions performed on women in their 30s and 40s than on women in their teens, according to the Canadian Institute for Health Information. More than half of those who terminate a pregnancy already have children. We represent the majority of women who access this medical service, so we should own our place in the abortion debate. This is why I'm telling my story. But before I shared it with Canadians, I had to tell my parents. I worked up to it at their home, where I grew up. "I need to tell you something," I said to them. "I had an abortion six years ago." Silence.

I am the eldest of five siblings. My mother almost never challenged me—she didn't question my decision to backpack across Europe as a teenager or, a decade later, to follow a doctor to Sri Lanka to write about his work when the country was on the brink of civil war. But this, I could see in her eyes, was very different. Abortion was acceptable in some circumstances, she agreed, but this wasn't one of them. I was stronger than I gave myself credit for, she said. I could have handled another child just fine. She said she'd been better off not knowing. I looked at my father. "That's life, I guess," he finally offered. A week later, my mother brought up the subject again. She wasn't troubled just by my abortion but by the fact I was willing to write about it under my name. She warned that I wasn't thinking clearly. When you're living in a small city, this decision will follow you everywhere, she said.

I'm a few years short of my 40th birthday. I don't really care what people think of me. But the woman who brought me into this world wasn't convinced. Her hurt was real, and I couldn't ignore that. And that's why, for some time, I struggled with whether to write this anony-mously. In the end, I used my own name. I understand why so many women stay silent, but I won't anymore. I don't feel ashamed. And if you see yourself in this story, neither should you. We've held our collective breath for too long. Let's begin to let it out together.

1. To many, the author might not fit the stereotype of a woman seeking an abortion. Yet in Canada, her age group has more abortions than teens. Is this statistic surprising? If so, why might this be the case?

2. Do you believe any particular demographic of abortion seekers is stigmatized more than others in America? If so, do you (like the author) see age and marital status as the key determining factors of stigmatization, or might race and class be more important?

"WELCOME TO SWEDEN: NOTES ON BIRTHDAY CONDOMS, HOME ABORTIONS, AND HYSTERICAL AMERICANS," BY INGRID ANDERSSON, FROM *THE PROGRESSIVE*, DECEMBER 4, 2015

I came to Sweden to research reproductive freedom. I wanted to study family policies in a country where citizens get 480 days of paid parental leave and up to six weeks of annual paid vacation and where, I had heard, the government mails birthday greetings and condoms to young people when they are considered old enough to have sex.

When I left the United States, where I am a home-birth midwife and an advocate for women's autonomy, reproductive freedom, and healthy families, the seemingly intractable conflicts over abortion, sex, and "family values" were raging. I thought getting out of the country might give me different perspectives and maybe even hope.

The first thing I notice, as a mother and midwife landing in Sweden, is the extraordinary attention paid to families. I discover that the narrow parallel tracks running up staircases, indoor and outdoor, are for strollers. I see strollers and wheelchairs everywhere, fitting into inviting and welcoming (beyond merely accommodating) public spaces. Every urban neighborhood has a grocery store stocked with real food that by law contains no unnecessary antibiotics, added hormones, corn syrup, or endocrine disrupting chemicals. Every neighborhood has a local health clinic and youth center.

There are no window decals prohibiting handguns, because Swedes don't carry them. (It is illegal for a civilian to carry a firearm here unless for a specific, legal purpose, such as hunting or attending a shooting range.) A public bench seems to pop up whenever my dysplastic hip needs one. Dedicated bike paths abound. I marvel at how cars stop for pedestrians and bikers at every zebra crossing, and it almost makes me weep. I have seen cars hit bikers and pedestrians in America, and an eleven-year-old boy was killed recently along the very same traffic corridor where my son walked to school (and about which neighbors and I complained for years). This feels bigger than family friendliness. This is flesh-and-blood, money-where-the-mouth-is striving for humane and inclusive quality of life.

I say "striving" because democracy is a dizzying business, riddled with argument and debate. The American in me balks at the 25 percent value-added tax, higher even than Norway's, as well as the "rules are rules" mentality that drives Swedish behavior. I cannot count how many times I've been told, "regler ar regler." For the first time in my life, I have been pulled over by police and asked to blow into a breathalyzer. And I never, ever fail to come to a dead halt at stop signs, because even on a vacant road there can be a traffic camera, and fines are steep.

But the American in me decides she is happy to pay high taxes and play by Swedish rules on the first day of public school.

My son's teacher said he did not need to bring anything apart from his curious, well-rested, breakfasted self. School will supply all his school needs, including an iPad and hot meals made from scratch. His first lunch—eaten over an hour at a round wooden table, sitting on a real wooden chair, in an actual dining room filled with windows and art—is baked salmon in rich cream sauce, dilled potatoes, steamed broccoli, salad with home-made dressing, bread, butter, and organic milk, served in all-you-can-eat buffet style. The kitchen uses 30 percent organic ingredients, locally produced when possible. My seventh grader is disoriented but delighted by trusting adults and an open campus with unlocked doors. (Every morning since Sandy Hook, my son's school in America was all locked up by the time the kids were reciting the Pledge of Allegiance.)

Three weeks after school starts, teachers, parents, and students in my son's class, all on a first-name basis, come together with the principals and play party games. Torsten and Kirsten, the co-principals, also show us a short new film about teenage brain development and apply it to teen relationships, screen time, food and beverage choices, exercise, and sleep. They tell us why there is zero tolerance for bullying, graffiti, and energy drinks and about the variety of skilled and safe on-site adults to whom our teens can turn. All evening, not a single condescending or disparaging word about adolescence is said or implied. Not a sign of weary adult forbearance is exhibited. We walk home feeling connected and energized.

With my child happy, settling into a school with which I could not feel more satisfied, I am free to go to work. I devour library articles and books and begin scheduling interviews.

A surprisingly moving, autobiographical comic book called *It Grows: An Illustrated Story of Abortion* and a simple story by a youth social worker called *The Secret* teach me in grounding terms how sex education, contraception, and abortion work in Sweden. Any Swedish teen or adult can walk into one of the common health centers and talk confidentially with a counselor or midwife about any personal or social issue or need, including pregnancy. She or he probably will already have been introduced to a youth health center on a school class field trip at age twelve or thirteen.

Youth and young adult health centers in Sweden offer a limitless supply of free condoms, free testing and treatment for chlamydia and other diseases, and free emergency contraception. Pregnant minors are encouraged but not required to involve a parent. Counselors and/or psychiatrists meet with girls and are available to all women. Abortion is free or low-cost and available on-demand up to eighteen weeks of pregnancy. A dating ultrasound is required, and if the pregnancy is earlier than three months, girls and women can choose between vacuum extraction or pill-induced abortion and to complete the abortion at home.

Abortions are performed up to twenty-two weeks of pregnancy, but after eighteen weeks there must be a medical indication and a psychiatrist is involved. All girls and women are encouraged to include support persons. Midwives, who are prescribing professionals associated with health and wellness, support all girls and women through normal pregnancy and birth, as well as contraception and abortion choices.

Records from ancient times to the present day indicate that women tend to prefer coping with unwanted pregnancy privately and using measures within their control, or within a circle of trusted family or friends. Preference for autonomy and privacy is evidenced even when clinic-mediated options are accessible. Thanks in part to research at Sweden's Karolinska Institutet, home abortion is now predictably safe and effective. For women from Stockholm to Nairobi, it has become a first-choice abortion method.

America stands as an exception. For American women, politically driven drug restrictions, costs, and lack of funding for education and support make obstacles to home abortion formidable.

The week I left home, one of my heroes in the struggle for women's reproductive freedom died. Anne Gaylor, a great American visionary and freethinker, quietly helped thousands of women get safe abortions before *Roe v. Wade* became the law of the land.

What began as a living room telephone support, education, and referral service connecting women and abortion providers in New York and Mexico grew into America's first private donor fund dedicated to helping women pay for abortions. Anne's work in reproductive freedom caused her to go on to found the Freedom From Religion Foundation.

Today, anti-abortionists in America continue to shape private and public discourse about abortion and erect ever more sophisticated barriers between women and empowering reproductive health care. Were it not for the tireless volunteers at Anne Gaylor's Women's Medical Fund, girls and women in my home state of Wisconsin might as well live in the pre-*Roe v. Wade* era. Anne summed it up this way: "Without the choice of abortion, women can't be free."

In Wisconsin, where I have attended births for over two decades, first in a hospital and then through my own home birth practice, women have begun contacting me for home abortion help. I helped them or someone they know through arguably greater risks, choices, responsibilities, and pains of pregnancy and birth. Can I help them end an unwanted pregnancy? The question seems perfectly natural.

Like all midwives, I have routine access to misoprostol, one of the two needed abortion pills and which cost me exactly ninety-eight cents apiece. But by most state laws, including my own, a doctor must deliver the pills. In Wisconsin, at least twenty-four hours prior to the abortion, a physician trained in surgical abortion must read a state-drafted script and perform or review a detailed ultrasound in the presence of each girl or woman, exactly as specified and mandated by the state. The girl or woman must attest by signature that these letters of the law were obeyed.

Can I go to Planned Parenthood, then, to be a support person in the process? Planned Parenthood does not allow doulas, for safety reasons, I'm told. Security is a serious issue. A nurse practitioner friend tells me she still hears, "He's got a gun! He's got a gun!" ringing in her ears from the day in the Planned Parenthood parking lot when (in a twist of abortion history) a man pulled out a loaded pistol and killed himself. His ex-girlfriend was having an abortion there that day.

At another Wisconsin clinic, an ever-present pick-eter dooms to hell everyone entering and exiting, while capturing them and their license plates on videotape. Some clinic staff regularly wear disguises, bullet-proof vests, and drive only rental cars to work. Some even choose not to vote, in fear of making their home addresses discoverable. An abortion physician friend of mine reports her relief whenever quiet, ho-hum picketers greet her in the morning. Such a state of affairs and worse, spanning the last four decades in America, is incomprehensible to the Swedes I interview.

"Publicly protesting abortion or anything related would be seen as hysterical in Sweden, not even the Christian party would do that!" says Ella, a twenty-eight-year-old hospital gynecology nurse who plans to continue studies to become a midwife.

Ella, who lived in Australia and traveled extensively, speaks excellent English. She is a Stockholm native and unmarried, until recently had a long-term partner, or "sarbo," meaning unmarried partner living separately.

This term is to be distinguished from "sambo," meaning unmarried live-in partner. Ella plans to have children when she meets the right man.

University tuition is free for Swedish citizens, daycare and preschool are subsidized, and every Swedish child receives a monthly stipend from the government of about $125 until age sixteen. Therefore Ella does not feel pressure to establish herself in her chosen profession before starting a family. She has never had an abortion and uses an IUD for contraception. "But most people use condoms until they know each other really well or are in a long-term relationship." She adds, "I would say Swedish parents tend to be older. Families tend to be smaller."

She tells me health professionals in Sweden are not allowed to "opt out" of supporting or prescribing emergency contraception or abortions. "This was actually tested recently by a midwife who wanted to refuse to prescribe abortion pills. She asked the Christian Democrat party for help. But the official ruling decided she had to perform her job properly, according to her job description, or find a different one."

Rules are rules.

What about picketers, threats, sabotaging tactics of the type used in America? Ella has no knowledge of any such activities. "It would be on the front page of all the newspapers for a week," she says. Sonja and Anneli shake their heads vigorously when I ask them the same question. "Never, women in Sweden will never go backwards that way," Sonja says. "That would be crazy!"

Sonja is a single, dynamic, forty-one-year-old actress from Kiruna, a "small, man-dominated mining town" in the far north of Sweden. Anneli is a fifty-six-year-old writer, mother of three adult children, and new grandmother from southern Sweden who fills the room with maternal warmth. "Abortion isn't controversial in Sweden, you know, because most Swedes do not have a religious belief against it," Anneli says.

I ask Anneli and Sonja how they feel about pill-induced abortion, which American abortion opponents have been working particularly hard to suppress. Anneli says two of her children have had pill-induced abortions. "Pill abortion is at home, a woman's body does it. It's hard, but it's meaningful. Everybody chooses this now unless it's too late." She felt proud of her children's partners, who showed strength in unity and support. In her mind, the partners had passed a sort of test for partnerhood and parenthood. Of her own history with a vacuum extraction abortion, Anneli says, "My abortion was done to me. I did nothing. It was really my doctor's abortion."

As a homebirth midwife and an advocate for empowering women, I find Anneli's perspective striking.

"I have never had an abortion," says Sonja, "but a woman shouldn't be given the idea she can't do it on her own." She continues, "No one sees abortion as a replacement for birth control. Nobody thinks, I'll just have sex and oh, oops, if I get pregnant I'll have an abortion. Being pregnant when it's not the right time is not fun for anybody." I wonder if she is thinking of another story she chooses not to share. "For me, it's 'no condom, no sex!' AIDS changed everything. Everybody uses condoms now."

But of course, sometimes condoms break, and even Swedes some times break the rules.

County governments in Sweden mailed birthday condoms to young people throughout the 1990s and early

2000s. In Stockholm County from 2004 until 2014, every twenty -three-year-old received a personal letter with information on sexual health and a condom.

Today, the birthday mailings have stopped, but there are free condoms everywhere—in churches, grocery stores, airports.

The Church of Sweden made national news when it distributed free condoms at a gay pride parade. "Condoms show that we protect life," explained church spokesperson Annika Nordequit. "It doesn't mean we encourage promiscuity." Every rainbow-colored packet of church condoms was emblazoned with the words, "Most important of all is love." Anneli says that public school nurses in Sweden teach sexual health and pregnancy prevention in detail. She describes her youngest son's class trip to the community health center as a kind of rite of passage. "When Niklas came home from his class trip to the health center, he was so proud of the condom he got there ... He showed it to me, and then carefully hid it away in his drawer." Anneli and Sonja say they were not able to have that kind of openness with their parents.

Sweden is not some static utopia. Attitudes and public policy have evolved here over time and are still evolving. As an American, I take that as a hopeful sign.

"It has changed so much, it's unbelievable and wonderful how much it's changed!" says Sonja. "I grew up in a remote, homophobic town way up north in Sweden. When I went home to visit last time, I didn't know where I was. I really could not believe I had grown up there.The hockey team was wearing rainbow colors to show support for gay rights. Everything had changed so much, I just cried."

Across Europe, there is a strong movement for

progress on equal rights.

This morning, a couple of hours south from where I sit, a history-making drone is flying from Germany across the Oder river to Slubice, Poland. Not a military drone, not a Google drone, it is operated by visionary, free-thinking women working with the Dutch group Women on Waves. They are finding a new route across political, economic, and religious divides. The drone carries abortion pills.

In Poland, where abortion is in most cases illegal, sex education is woefully inadequate and contraception severely restricted. Despite its illegality, abortion takes place regularly and is a class issue. Affluent Polish women can obtain abortions in Vienna or London. Empowered Polish women can maneuver around sinister Right to Life traps and pay for an illegal abortion in Poland. Today's drone is meant to spotlight Poland's rural and working-class women, and how women's bodies remain a battlefield, even in Europe.

Anneli is currently researching her grandmother's life story. A timeworn reality of inescapable hardships and cruel inequalities is not so long ago or far away. Beneath our feet, in fact, righteous domination, disparities, and disease wore women out, physically and mentally, claimed lives of mothers and children, and forced fear into normal, loving people of all ages.

I recently came upon an old Swedish postal stamp that symbolizes Sweden's pledge of allegiance to children, families, and quality of life for all. It appeared in 1980.

The stamp depicts Elise Ottesen-Jensen, 1886-1973, a tireless soldier for reproductive rights who, like Anne Gaylor, looked realities in the face and fought from living rooms, newspaper pages, courtrooms and stages to defend freedoms of mind and body. Like Anne, she ran a volunteer abortion referral service. Ottesen-Jensen gazes out from the stamp with a humble, head-tipped expression similar to Gaylor's. Even the quotation could be Anne's:

I dream of that day, when all children born are welcome, all men and women are equal, and sexuality is an expression of intimacy, pleasure, and tenderness.

1. Sweden is often lauded as a bastion of progressivism, but skeptics point out that it is a small and homogenous country, nothing like America. Based on this report, how might Sweden be an example for pro-choice Americans?

2. Do you think Sweden's government is too involved with young adults' sex lives? Or is this appropriate?

CONCLUSION

Abortion has been an option for women seeking to terminate an unwanted pregnancy since ancient times. Generally speaking, an abortion within the first trimester of a pregnancy has not been considered murder, though it has met with varying degrees of legality and societal approval.

In the United States, abortion was illegal everywhere by 1965, except in cases where the pregnancy endangered the mother's life, or in cases of rape or incest. In 1973, the Supreme Court reversed this with the landmark *Roe v. Wade* decision. This provided Constitutional protection for the legal right to an abortion. Although the high court's decision gave states some leeway to legislate abortion, it was nonetheless understood as a critical victory for women's reproductive rights, and a welcome goodbye to the days of illegal and unsafe abortions.

Since *Roe*, opponents of abortion have worked tirelessly to reverse the ruling and restrict access to abortion, turning a woman's private decision into one of society's most divisive issues. The so-called "pro-life" movement acts on the deeply held moral conviction that abortion is murder. A host of additional reasons are cited to support this view. Some of these, such as an alleged link between abortion and breast cancer, have been debunked. However, high rates of abortion among women of color cause some concern. To link abortion demographic data to eugenic ideology may be a stretch, but such accusations are more difficult to dismiss than those based on faulty science.

Both 2015 and 2016 were ambitious years for abortion opponents. The various attempts to roll back *Roe* covered earlier in this volume are a testament to the tenacity of the pro-life position, as it struggles against the perceived bias of the liberal media, and majority public opinion. The 2016 presidential election also had great consequences for the pro-choice movement, with many opponents of *Roe v. Wade* taking key government positions. The battle for reproductive rights continues to be waged. For this reason, it is crucial to have accurate and up-to-date information about abortion. It is our hope this reader has provided this.

BIBLIOGRAPHY

Ahluwalia, Sanjam. "Abortion and Gay Marriage: Sexual Modernity and Its Dissonance in the Contemporary World." *Economic & Political Weekly*, Volume 50, Issue 50, December 21, 2015, pp. 27-30.

Andersson, Ingrid. "Welcome To Sweden: Notes On Birthday Condoms, Home Abortions, And Hysterical Americans." *The Progressive*, December 2015. http://www.progressive.org /news/2015/12/188447/welcome-sweden-notes-birthday-condoms-home-abortions-and-hysterical-americans.

Anderson, Ryan T. "The Roe Of Marriage: Traditionalists Should Defend Their Conception Of The Truth." *National Review*, Auguat 11, 2014. https://www.nationalreview.com/nrd/articles/383581/roe-marriage.

Brown, Simon. "Barrier Method? U.S. Supreme Court To Hear New Group Of Cases That Could Further Limit Americans' Access To Reproductive Health Care." *Church and State*, January 2016. https://www.au.org/church-state/january-2016 -church-state/featured/barrier-method.

Callahan, David. "Who's Who At The Secretive Susan Thompson Buffett Foundation?" *Inside Philanthropy*, February 4, 2014. http://www.insidephilanthropy.com/home/2014/2/4/whos-who -at-the-secretive-susan-thompson-buffett-foundation.html.

Dreweke, Joerg. "New Clarity For The U.S. Abortion Debate: A Steep Drop In Unintended Pregnancy Is Driving Recent Abortion Declines." *Guttmacher Policy Review*, Volume 19, Issue 1, 2016, pp. 16-22. https://www.guttmacher.org/about/gpr/2016/03 /new-clarity-us-abortion-debate-steep-drop-unintended-pregnancy-driving-recent.

Forsythe, Clarke. "How the Next President Can Protect Human Life." *National Review*, June 20, 2016. http://www.nationalreview.com/article/436809/pro-life-measures-next-president -must-take.

Landecker, Heidi. "As States Try to Curb Abortion, Future Doctors Fight for Training." *The Chronicle of Higher Education*, June 21, 2013. http://www.chronicle.com/article/As-States-Try-to -Curb/139831.

"Lies in the Exam Room." *Women's Health Activist,* September 9. 2016. https://www.nwhn.org/lies-exam-room.

Martin, Nina. "Amid Abortion Debate, the Pursuit of Science." *ProPublica,* January 7, 2014. https://www.propublica.org/article/amid-abortion-debate-the-pursuit-of-science.

– – –. "Behind the Supreme Court's Abortion Decision, More Than a Decade of Privately Funded Research." *ProPublica,* July 14, 2016. https://www.propublica.org/article/supreme-court-abortion-decision-more-than-decade-privately-funded-research.

– – –. "7 Reproductive Rights Issues to Watch in 2015." *ProPublica,* January 16, 2015. https://www.propublica.org/article/7-reproductive-rights-issues-to-watch-in-2015.

Messerly, John G. "Ethicists Generally Agree: The Pro-Life Arguments Are Worthless." *Reason and Meaning,* May 17, 2016. http://ieet.org/index.php/IEET/more/Messerly20160517.

NARAL. "Abortion Bans Endanger Women's Health." *NARAL. org.* http://www.prochoiceamerica.org/media/fact-sheets/abortion-bans-no-exceptions-endanger-women.pdf.

Ornstein, Charles, "Activists Pursue Private Abortion Details Using Public Records Laws." *ProPublica,* August 25, 2015. https://www.propublica.org/article/activists-pursue-private-abortion-details-using-public-records-laws.

Riddick, Ruth. "Grandma's Matrilineal Road Trip: A Conversation Across Generations." *Conscience and Catholics for Choice,* Spring 2016. http://consciencemag.org/2016/04/25/grandmas-matrilineal-road-trip-a-conversation-across-generations.

Singh, Dipti. "At The Court: Women's Rights At Stake." *Women's Health Activist,* May-June 2016. https://www.nwhn.org/court-womens-rights-stake.

Sission, Gretchen and Renee Bracey Sherman. "Illegal Abortions Onscreen: Depictions of a Pre-'Roe' World." *Rewire,* January 21, 2016. https://rewire.news/article/2016/01/21/illegal-abortions-onscreen-depictions-pre-roe-world.

Stradiotto, Laura. "Not the Right Time." *Chatelaine*, September 2016. http://www.chatelaine.com/living/choices/abortion-in-my-30s.

Sussman, Rachel. "The Landscape Of State Anti-Abortion Legislation." *Columbia Journal of Gender and Law*, Volume 29, Issue 1, 2015. http://cjgl.cdrs.columbia.edu/article/the-lan dscape-of-state-anti-abortion-legislation.

Thomas, Trevor. "Tim Kaine's Abortion Distortions." *American Thinker*, October 9, 2016. http://www.americanthinker.com/articles/2016/10/tim_kaines_abortion_distortions.html.

Yoder, Katie. "Top 10 Ways Media Spin Abortion as 'Moral,' 'Social Good.'" *NewsBusters*, Oct. 2014. http://www.newsbusters.org /blogs/katie-yoder/2014/10/23/top-10-ways-media-spin-abortion-moral-social-good.

CHAPTER NOTES

CHAPTER 1: WHAT ACADEMICS, EXPERTS, AND RESEARCHERS SAY

"NEW CLARITY FOR THE U.S. ABORTION DEBATE: A STEEP DROP IN UNINTENDED PREGNANCY IS DRIVING RECENT ABORTION DECLINES" BY JOERG DREWEKE

(1.) Blue M, Sensenbrenner: If we fund Planned Parenthood, how will we feed starving children?, *Right Wing Watch*, Sept. 9, 2015, http:// www.rightwingwatch.org/content/sensenbrenner-if-we-fund-planned -parenthood-how-will-we-feed-starving-children.

(2.) Jones RK and Jerman J, Abortion incidence and service availability in the United States, 2011, *Perspectives on Sexual and Reproductive Health*, 2014, 46(1):3-14, http://www.guttmacher .org/pubs/journals/ psrh.46e0414.pdf.

(3.) Doeflinger R, On abortion rates: good news and cause for reflection, *The Witherspoon Institute: Public Discourse*, Feb. 10, 2014, http://www.thepublicdiscourse.com/2014/02/12052.

(4.) Americans United for Life, Guttmacher Institute fails to acknowledge the impact of pro-life legislation even as it reports Big Abortion's decline, notes Americans United for Life, Jan. 31, 2014, http://www.aul.org/2014/01/guttmacher-in stitute-fails-to-acknowledge -the-impact-of-pro-life-legislation -even-as-it-reports-big-abortions-decline -notes-americans -united-for-life.

(5.) Ertelt S, Abortion rate drops to its lowest level since 1973 as more babies saved from abortion, *LifeNews.com*, Feb. 3, 2014, http://www. lifenews.com/2014/02/03/abortion-rate-drops-to -its-lowest-level-since -1973-as-more-babies-saved-from-abortion.

(6.) Finer LB and Zolna MR, Declines in unintended pregnancy in the United States, 2008-2011, *The New England Journal of Medicine*, 2016, 374(9):843-852.

(7.) Mena A, Lower abortion rate credited to culture shift, not contraception, *Catholic News Agency*, Feb. 5, 2014, http://www .catholicnewsagency.com/news/ lower-abortion-rate-credit- ed-to-culture-shift-not-contraception/.

(8.) Chandra A et al, Sexual behavior, sexual attraction, and sexual identity in the United States: data from the 2006-2008 National Survey of Family Growth, *National Health Statistics Reports*, Hyattsville, MD: National Center for Health Statistics, 2011, No. 36, http://www.cdc.gov.libproxy.unm.edu/ nchs/data/nhsr/nhsr036.pdf.

(9.) National Center for HIV/AIDS, Viral Hepatitis, STD, and TB Prevention, Centers for Disease Control and Prevention, Trends in the prevalence of sexual behaviors and HIV testing, national YRBS: 1991-2013, no date, http://www.cdc.gov.libproxy.unm.edu/healthyyouth/data/yrbs/pdf/trends/us_sexual_trend_ yrbs.pdf.

(10.) Frost JJ, Zolna MR and Frohwirth L, *Contraceptive Needs and Services, 2012 Update*, New York: Guttmacher Institute, 2014, http://www.guttmacher.org/pubs/win/contraceptive-needs-2012.pdf.

(11.) Passel JS, Cohn D and Lopez MH, Hispanics account for more than half of nation's growth in past decade, *Pew Research Center*, 2011, http://www.pewhispanic.org/2011/03/24/ hispanics-account-for-more-than-half-of-nations-growth-in-past-decade/.

(12.) Daniels K, Daugherty J and Jones J, Current contraceptive status among women aged 15-44: United States, 201 1-2013, *NCHS Data Brief*, Washington, DC: U.S. Department of Health and Human Services, 2014, No. 173, http://www.cdc.gov.libproxy.unm.edu/nchs/data/databriefs/db173.pdf.

(13.) Jones J, Mosher WD and Daniels K, Current contraceptive use in the United States, 2006-2010, and changes in patterns of use since 1995, *National Health Statistics Reports*, Hyattsville, MD: National Center for Health Statistics, 2012, No. 60, http://www.cdc.gov.libproxy.unm.edu/nchs/ data/nhsr/nhsr060.pdf.

(14.) Sonfield A, Hasstedt K and Gold RB, *Moving Forward: Family Planning in the Era of Health Reform*, New York: Guttmacher Institute, 2014, http://www.guttmacher.org/pubs/family-planning-and-healthreform.pdf.

(15.) Kavanaugh ML, Jerman J and Finer LB, Changes in use of long-acting reversible contraceptive methods among U.S. women, 20092012, *Obstetrics & Gynecology*, 2015, 126(5):917-927.

(16.) Boonstra HD, What is behind the declines in teen pregnancy rates?, *Guttmacher Policy Review*, 2014, 17(3):15-21, http://www.guttmacher. org/pubs/gpr/17/3/gpr170315.pdf.

(17.) Crary D, Abortions declining greatly across most of US, *Boston Globe*, June 8, 2015, http://www.bostonglobe.com

/news/ nation/2015/06/07/exclusive-abortions-declining-nearly-all-states/ DNRxPWSUBMVEq9J7rj6zbI/story.html.

(18.) Pazol K, Creanga AA and Jamieson DJ, Abortion surveillance—United States, 2012, *Morbidity and Mortality Weekly Report*, 2015, Vol. 44, No. 10, http://www.cdc.gov.libproxy.unm .edu/mmwr/pdf/ss/ss6410.pdf.

(19.) Henshaw SK et al., Restrictions on Medicaid Funding for Abortions: A Literature Review, New York: Guttmacher Institute, 2009, http://www. guttmacher.org/pubs/MedicaidLitReview.pdf.

(20.) Joyce TJ et al., *The Impact of State Mandatory Counseling and Waiting Period Laws on Abortion: A Literature Review*, New York: Guttmacher Institute, 2009, http://www.guttmacher.org/pubs / MandatoryCounseling.pdf.

(21.) Boonstra HD and Nash E, A surge of state abortion restrictions puts providers—and the women they serve—in the crosshairs, *Guttmacher Policy Review*, 2014, 17(1):9-15, http://www .guttmacher.org/pubs/ gpr/17/1/gpr170109.pdf.

(22.) Dreweke J, U.S. abortion rate continues to decline while debate over means to the end escalates, *Guttmacher Policy Review*, 2014, 17(2):2-7, http://www.guttmacher.org/pubs /gpr/17/2/gpr170202.pdf.

(23.) Grossman D et al., Change in abortion services after implementation of a restrictive law in Texas, *Contraception*, 2014, 90(5):496-501.

(24.) Guttmacher Institute, Fewer U.S. women of reproductive age were uninsured in 2014, news release, Sept. 22, 2015, http:// www. guttmacher.org/media/inthenews/2015/09/22/index.html.

(25.) Bearak et al., Changes in out-of-pocket costs for hormonal IUDs after implementation of the Affordable Care Act: an analysis of insurance benefit inquiries, *Contraception*, 2015, http://dx.doi.org.libproxy.unm.edu/10.1016/j.contraception.2015.08.018.

(26.) Sonfield A et al., Impact of the federal contraceptive coverage guarantee on out-of-pocket payments for contraceptives: 2014 update, *Contraception*, 2014, 91(1):44-48, http://www.contraceptionjournal.org/ article/S0010-7824(14)00687-8/pdf.

(27.) IMS Institute for Healthcare Informatics, *Medicine Use and Shifting Costs of Healthcare*, 2014, http://www.plannedparenthoodadvocate. org/2014/IIHI_US_Use_of_Meds_for_2013.pdf.

(28.) Guttmacher Institute, More state abortion restrictions were enacted in 201 1-2013 than in the entire previous decade, news release, Jan. 2, 2014, http://www.guttmacher.org/media/inthe-news/2014/01/02/index. html.

(29.) Hasstedt K, How Texas lawmakers continue to undermine women's health, *Health Affairs Blog*, May 20, 2015, http:// healthaffairs.org.libproxy.unm.edu/blog/2015/05/20/ how-tex-as-lawmakers-continue-to-undermine-womens-health/.

(30.) Frost J and Hasstedt K, Quantifying Planned Parenthood's critical role in meeting the need for publicly supported contra-ceptive care, *Health Affairs Blog*, Sept. 8, 2015, http://healthaf-fairs.org.libproxy.unm.edu/ blog/2015/09/08 /quantifying-planned-parenthoods-critical-role-in-meet-ing-the-need-for-publicly-supported-contraceptive-care/.

"ABORTION AND GAY MARRIAGE: SEXUAL MODERNITY AND ITS DISSONANCE IN THE CONTEMPORARY WORLD," BY SANJAM AHLUWALIA

1. Many scholars have addressed internal contradictions marking contemporary sexual politics, presenting compelling argu-ments about the limits of sexual modernity around gay politics. For details, see Massad (2002); Puar (2011); Najmabadi (2011); Ahmed (2011); Shakry and Paul Amar (2013).
2. Hobby Lobby is a US corporation that was allowed by the US Supreme Court decision in 2014 to refuse contraceptive cov-erage in their employees' healthcare plans, this despite there being a clause for preventive coverage under the Affordable Care Act. See Fuller (2014). For the implications of this ruling, also see Carroll (2014).
3. The text of the bill can be accessed electronically: http://www.gpo. gov/fdsys/pkg/BILLS-112hr3541ih/pdf/BILLS-112hr3541ih.pdf; also see Musial (2014).
4. See lines 15-20 of the bill "...some Americans are exercising sex-se-lection abortion practices within the United States consistent with discriminatory practices common to their country of origin, or the country to which they trace their ancestry." http://www.gpo. gov/fdsys/pkg/BILLS-112hr3541ih/pdf/BILLS-112hr3541ih.pdf

5. Large anti-abortion racist billboards went up in New York City; for details see Daily Mail (2011).
6. For feminist discussion on the Indian context see John (2014); Kaur (2008); Menon (2012).
7. Menon (2012) provides a careful and nunaced feminist reading of sex-selection abortions in India. I draw upon her argument here; for details see, "Abortion as a Feminist Issue."

CHAPTER 2: WHAT THE GOVERNMENT AND POLITICIANS SAY

THE LANDSCAPE OF STATE ANTI-ABORTION LEGISLATION" BY RACHEL SUSSMAN

1. *Planned Parenthood at a Glance*, Planned Parenthood, http://www.plannedparenthood.org/about-us/ who-we-are/planned-parenthood-at-a-glance [http://perma.cc/BFL9-BDMN] (last visited July 19, 2014).
2. *See New* Abortion *Restrictions: Arizona Women Have Fewer Health Care Options*, Planned Parenthood (Aug. 18, 2011), http://www.plannedparenthood.org/planned-parenthood-arizona/news-room/press-releases/ new-abortion-restrictions-arizona-women-have-fewer-health-care-options [http://perma.ee/334R-V6W6].
3. Bebe J. Anderson, *Litigating* Abortion *Access Cases in the Post-Windsor World*, 29 Colum. J. Gender & L. 143 (2015).
4. *See, e.g.*, Editorial, *Real Goal of* Abortion *'Limits Bans*, N.Y. Times (May 10, 2014), http://www.nytimes. com/2014/05/11/opinion /sunday/real-goal-of-abortion-limits-bans.html [http://perma. cc/W79G-FRDK].
5. *See, e.g.*, James MacPherson, *North Dakota Appeals After Judge Overturns Law that Bans Abortions If Fetal Heartbeat Detected*, U.S. News (May 14, 2014, 5:19 PM), http://www.usnews.com/news/us/ articles/2014/05/14/nd-appealing-judges-ruling-on-6-week-abortion-ban [http://perma.cc/9YG2-V9S2] (six-week ban); Arkansas Approves Strictest Abortion Ban in US, BBC (Mar. 7, 2013, 11:53 AM), http://www.bbc. com/news/world-us-canada-21705086 [http://perma.cc/VQ83-C42W] (twelve-weekban).

6. *See* Paige Winfield Cunningham, *Push Continues for 20-Week Abortion Ban*, Politico (Feb. 14,2014,1:31 PM), http://www.politico.com/story/2014/02/push-continues-for-20-week -abortion-bans-103535.html [http:// perma.cc/JQ72-2R7E].

7. *See Mandatory Waiting Period and Information Requirements for Women Seeking* Abortions, Kaiser Family Found., http://kff.org /womens-health-policy/state-indicator/mandatory-waiting-periods/ [http://perma. cc/M7LR-9K5D] (last visited July 19, 2014).

8. *See, e.g., Refusal to Provide Medical Services*, NARAL Pro-Choice Am., http://www.prochoiceamerica. org/what-is-choice/fast -facts/refusal-to-provide-medical.html [http://perma.cc/8ZDF-DMN3] (last visited July 19, 2014); Reid Wilson, Mississippi Passes Arizona-Style Religious Freedom Bill, Wash. Post (Apr. 1, 2014), http://www.washingtonpost.com/blogs/govbeat /wp/2014/04/01/mississippi-passes-arizona-style-religiousfre edom-bill/ [http://perma.cc/6EE2-4VCR].

9. *See* Roe v. Wade *at 40: Most Oppose Overturning* Abortion *Decision*, Pew Research: Religion & Pub. Life Project (Jan. 16, 2013), http://www.pewforum.org/2013/01/16/roe-v-wade-at-40/ [http:// perma.cc/6BMG-8QAB1.

10. *See* Fernanda Santos, *Arizona Governor Vetoes Bill on Refusal of Service to Gays*, N.Y. Times (Feb. 26, 2014), http://www.nytimes .com/2014/02/27/us/Brewer-arizona-gay-service-bill.html [http://perma.cc/S9P-MX5T].

11. *See* Aaron Blake & Rachel Weiner, *Ohio Repeals Law Restricting Unions; Miss. Blocks Personhood 'Amendment*, Wash. Post (Nov. 8, 2011), http://www.washingtonpost.com/politics/govemors-rac-es-pale-nextto-issues-votes- in-miss-ohio/2011/11/08 /gIQAbtiP3M_story.html [http://perma.ee/6DFF-VX4Y].

12. *See* Michael Muskal, *Missouri Is Latest Battleground over* Abortion *Rights*, Restrictions, L.A. Times (May 15, 2014, 9:37 AM), http://www.latimes.com/nation/nationnow/la-na-nn-abortion-missouri-20140515story.html [http://perma. cc/927Y-N9R7].

13. *See* Cathi Herrod at *Helm of Conservative Center for Arizona Policy, Guiding Lawmakers*, Ariz. Daily Sun (Mar. 2, 2014, 7:30 AM), http://azdailysun.com/news/local/state-and-regional/cathi-herrod-at-helm-of-conservative- center-for-arizona-policy /article_fabe26a2-alba-11 e3-9a43-0019bb2963f4.html [http:// perma. cc/LY7F-44AK].

CRITICAL PERSPECTIVES ON ABORTION

CHAPTER 3: WHAT THE COURTS SAY

"AT THE COURT: WOMEN'S RIGHTS AT STAKE" BY DIPTI SINGH

1. *Whole Woman's Health v. Hellerstedt*, Case No. 15-274 (S. Ct. 2016).
2. *See Planned Parenthood of Southeastern Pennsylvania v. Casey*, 505 U.S. 833, 845-46 (1992).
3. *Id.* at 846, 877-78.
4. *See* Brief of Amici Curiae ACOG et al., *Whole Woman's Health v. Cole*, Case No. 15-274 (Oct. 5, 2015).
5. Elizabeth Nash et al., Guttmacher Institute, *Laws Affecting Reproductive Health and Rights: 2015 State Policy Review*, available at http://www.guttmacher.org/statecenter/updates/2015/statetrends42015.html.
6. Nos. 14-1418, 14-1453, 14-1505, 15-35, 15-105, 15-119, & 15-19.
7. Religious Freedom Restoration Act of 1993, 42 U.S.C. §§2000bb *et seq*.
8. Laurie Sobel & Alina Salganicoff, Kaiser Family Foundation, *Issue Brief: Contraceptive Coverage at the Supreme Court Zubik v. Burwell: Does the Law Accommodate or Burden Nonprofits' Religious Beliefs?* (Feb. 2016, Updated Mar. 2016).
- See more at: https://www.nwhn.org/court-womens-rights-stake/#sthash.sGCLDEE2.dpuf

CHAPTER 4: WHAT ADVOCACY GROUPS SAY

"ABORTION BANS ENDANGER WOMEN'S HEALTH" FROM NATIONAL ABORTION AND REPRODUCTIVE RIGHTS ACTION LEAGUE (NARAL)

1. *Roe v. Wade*, 410 U.S. 113 (1973).
2. S.Amdt. 3083 to H.R.1833, Roll Call Vote 593, 104th Cong. (1995); S.Amdt 288 to H.R.1122, Roll Call Vote 69, 105th Cong. (1997); S.Amdt 289 to H.R.1122, Roll Call Vote 70, 105th

Cong. (1997); S.Amdt. 2319 to S.1692, Roll Call Vote 335, 106th Cong. (1999); H.R.1122, Roll Call Vote 63, 105th Cong. (1997); H.R.1122, Roll Call Vote 64, 105th Cong. (1997); H.R.3660, Roll Call Vote 103, 106th Cong. (2000); H.R.4965, Roll Call Vote 342, 107th Cong. (2002); S.Amdt. 258 to S. 3, Roll Call Vote 45, 108th Cong. (2003); S. 3 Roll Call Vote 47, 108th Cong. (2003); S.Amdt. 260 to S. 3, Roll Call Vote 48, 108th Cong. (2003); S.Amdt. 259 to S. 3, Roll Call Vote 46, 108th Cong. (2003); S.Amdt. 261 to S. 3, Roll Call Vote 49, 108th Cong. (2003); H.Amdt. 154 to H.R.760, Roll Call Vote 240, 108th Cong. (2003); H.R.760, Roll Call Vote 241, 108th Cong. (2003).

3. Catholic Bishops' Statement on Partial Birth Abortion (Oct. 2000), *at* http://www.priestsforlife.org/magisterium/bish-ops/00-10bpspba.htm (last visited Dec. 10, 2015); Americans United For Life, *Trojan Horse "Health" Exception Used To Strike Down Partial Birth Abortion Ban* (Sept. 8, 2004), *on file with* NARAL Pro-Choice America; American Life League, *Protecting the Life of the Mother…,* at http://www.all.org/get-involved/activist-materials/declaration-protecting-the-life-of-themother/ (last visited Dec. 10, 2015); American Life League, *Declaration: Protecting the Mother: List* [List of Doctors Who Have Pledged That Abortion Is Never Necessary to Save the Life of the Mother] (Aug. 8, 2007), at http://www.all.org/get involved/activist-materials/protecting-the-life-of-the-motherdeclaration-list/ (last visited Dec. 10, 2015).

4. In 2009 and 2010, President Obama had the opportunity to appoint two new justices to the court, Justice Sonia Sotomayor, replacing Justice Souter, and Justice Elena Kagan, replacing Justice Stevens. Neither justice has a record on choice and thus their position if a challenge to *Roe* were to come before the court remains to be seen.

5. *Gonzales v. Carhart and Gonzales v. Planned Parenthood Federation of America*, 127 S. Ct. 1610 (2007).

6. See Also: NARAL Pro-Choice America, *Fact Sheet: The Federal Abortion Ban* at http://www.prochoiceamerica.org/media/fact-sheets/abortion-bans-federal-abortion-ban.pdf (last visited Dec. 10, 2015).

7. Partial-Birth Abortion Ban Act of 2003, 18 U.S.C.A. § 1531 (2003).

8. *Roe v. Wade*, 410 U.S. 113 (1973).

9. *Doe v. Bolton*, 410 U.S. 179 (1973).

10. *Planned Parenthood of Southeastern Pennsylvania v. Casey*, 505 U.S. 833 (1992).

11. *Stenberg v. Carhart*, 530 U.S. 914 (2000).
12. *Stenberg*, 530 U.S. at 931.
13. *Stenberg*, 530 U.S. at 937.
14. *Ayotte v. Planned Parenthood of N. New England*, 390 F.3d 53 (1st Cir. 2004), cert. granted, 544 U.S. 1048 (May 23, 2005) (No. 04-1144).
15. *Ayotte v. Planned Parenthood of N. New England*, 546 U.S. 320 (2006).
16. H.B. 184, 1st Year, 160th Sess., Gen. Ct. (N.H. 2007).
17. 2011 N.H. Laws 205.
18. *Gonzales v. Carhart and Gonzales v. Planned Parenthood Federation of America*, 127 S.Ct. 1610 (2007).
19. *Carhart/PPFA*, 127 S.Ct. at 1634.
20. Telis Demos, *Not Black-and-White: Most Americans Back Health Exception to 'Partial-Birth' Abortion Ban*, ABCNEWS.COM, July 24, 2003, at http://abcnews.go.com/sections/living/goodmorningamerica/poll030724_abortion.html (last visited Dec. 10, 2015).
21. Partial Birth Abortion Ban of 1995: Hearing on H.R.1833/S. 939 Before the Senate Comm. on the Judiciary, 104th Cong. (1995) (testimony of Vikki Stella).
22. Judy Foreman, *When Drugs Are The Only Choice For A Mother-To-Be*, Sept. 26, 2000, at http://judyforeman.com/columns/when-drugs-are-only-choice-mother-be (last visited Dec. 10, 2015).
23. The National Cancer Institute, U.S. National Institutes of Health, *General Information About Breast Cancer Treatment and Pregnancy* (Dec. 3, 2010), at http://www.cancer.gov/cancertopics/pdq/treatment/breastcancer-and pregnancy/HealthProfessional (last visited Dec. 10, 2015).
24. Tommy Craggs, *Between a Woman's Heart and Head: Health vs. a Baby Is Just One Dilemma Faced By Heart Patients*, KANSAS CITY STAR, Nov. 7, 2000, at E1.
25. *Drug Fear Endangers Pregnant Women: Many Aren't Taking Medicine They Need*, USA TODAY, Dec. 12, 2000
26. Lisa Nainggolan, *Pregnant Pause: Evaluating Pregnant Women with Heart Disease* (Dec. 24, 2003), at http://www.medscape.com/viewarticle/782854 (last visited Dec. 10, 2015).
27. Jason Clayworth, *Her Baby Wasn't Expected to Live, But Nebraska Law Banned Abortion*, DES MOINES REGISTER, Mar. 6, 2011.

28. Press Release, National Abortion Federation, *Statement of Christy Zink on Harmful Impact of HR 3803* (Feb. 21, 2012) at http://prochoice.org/statement-of-christy-zink-on-harmful-impact-of-hr-3803/ (last visited Nov. 3, 2014).
29. Partial Birth Abortion Ban of 1995: Hearing on H.R.1833 Before the House Comm. on the Judiciary, Subcomm. on the Constitution, 104th Cong. (1996) (testimony of Coreen Constello).
30. *Partial Birth Abortion Ban of 1995: Hearing on H.R.1833/S. 939 Before the Senate Comm. on the Judiciary*, 104th Cong. (1995) (testimony of Tammy Watts).
31. *Partial Birth Abortion Ban of 1995: Hearing on H.R.1833/S. 939 Before the Senate Comm. on the Judiciary*, 104th Cong. (1995) (testimony of Tammy Watts).
32. *Partial Birth Abortion Ban of 1995: Hearing on H.R.1833/S. 939 Before the Senate Comm. on the Judiciary*, 104th Cong. (1995) (testimony of Viki Wilson).
33. *Planned Parenthood of Southeastern Pennsylvania v. Casey*, 505 U.S. 833 (1992).
34. *Carhart/PPFA*, 127 S. Ct. 1610 (2007).
35. States with laws banning so-called "partial-birth" abortion or other abortion procedures are: AL, AK, AZ, AR, FL, GA, ID, IL, IN, IA, KS, KY, LA, MI, MS, MO, NE, NH, NJ, ND, OH, OK, RI, SC, SD, TN, UT, VA, WV, WI. NARAL Pro-Choice America & NARAL Pro-Choice America Foundation, *Who Decides?: The Status of Women's Reproductive Rights in the United States* (24rd ed. 2015), available at www.WhoDecides.org.
36. These states are: AL, AK, AZ, AR, FL, GA, ID, IL, IN, IA, KS, KY, LA, MI, MS, MO, NE, NH, NJ, ND, OK, RI, SC, SD, TN, UT, VA, WV, WI. NARAL Pro-Choice America & NARAL Pro-Choice America Foundation, *Who Decides?: The Status of Women's Reproductive Rights in the United States* (26th ed. 2016), available at www.WhoDecides.org.
37. *Richmond Med. Ctr. v. Herring*, Nos. 03-1821, 04-1255, 2009 WL 1783515 (4th Cir. June 24, 2009).
38. See Victor G. Rosenblum & Thomas J. Marzen, *Strategies for Reversing* Roe v. Wade *Through the Courts*, in ABORTION AND THE CONSTITUTION, REVERSING *ROE V. WADE* THROUGH THE COURTS 198 (Dennis J. Horan et al. eds., 1987).

CHAPTER 5: WHAT THE MEDIA SAY

"LIES IN THE EXAM ROOM" FROM WOMEN'S HEALTH ACTIVIST, A NEWSLETTER FOR THE NATIONAL WOMEN'S HEALTH NETWORK

1. Schulz KF, Grimes DA, "Case-control studies: research in reverse," Lancet 2002; 359(9304): 431-434. doi:10.1016/S0140-6736 (02)07605-5.
2 .Susan G Komen Foundation, Abortion and Breast Cancer Risk, http://ww5.komen.org/BreastCancer/Table25Abortionan dbreastcancerrisk.html
3. Huang Y, Zhang X, Li W, et. al., "A meta-analysis of the association between induced abortion and breast cancer risk among Chinese females," Cancer Causes Control 2014; 25(2): 227-36. doi: 10.1007/s10552-013-0325-7. Epub 2013 Nov 24.
4. American College of Obstetricians and Gynecologists (ACOG), "Induced Abortion and Breast Cancer Risk. ACOG Committee Opinion No. 434." Obstet Gynecol 2009; 113: 1417–8. Available online at: http://www.acog.org/Resources_And_Publications /Committee_Opinions/Committee_on_Gynecologic_Practice /Induced_Abortion_and_Breast_Cancer_Risk.
5. Melbye M, Wohlfahrt J, Olsen JH, "Induced abortion and the risk of breast cancer," N Engl J Med 1997; 336: 81-85. doi: 10.1056/NEJM199701093360201..
6. Michels KB, Fei Xue MD, Colditz GA, et al., "Induced and spontaneous abortion and incidence of breast cancer among young women: a prospective cohort study," JAMA 2007; 167:814-820.
7. Henderson, KD, Sullivan-Halley J, Reynolds P, et. al., "Incomplete pregnancy is not associated with breast cancer risk: the California teachers study," 2008; 77(6):391-6. doi: 10.1016/j. contraception.2008.02.004. Epub 2008 Apr 18.
8. Beral, V, Bull D, "Breast cancer and abortion: collaborative reanalysis of data from 53 epidemiological studies, including 83 000 women with breast cancer from 16 countries," Lancet

2004; 363 (9414): 1007-016. Available online at: http://www.ncbi. nlm.nih.gov/pubmed/15051280.

9. National Cancer Institute (NCI), Abortion, Miscarriage, and Breast Cancer Risk, Bethesda MD: NCI, January 12, 2010.

10. National Breast Cancer Coalition (NBCC), Abortion and Breast Cancer Risk: Position Statement, Washington, DC: NBCC, Updated June 2010.

11. https://www.guttmacher.org/state-policy/explore/ove rview-abortion-laws

12. https://www.guttmacher.org/sites/default/files/pdfs/spibs /spib_MWPA.pdf

13. http://urge.org/wp-content/uploads/2015/08/Mandatory-De- lays-and-Counseling.pdf

14. http://repository.law.umich.edu/mjgl/vol19/iss1/1/?utm _source=repository.law.umich.edu%2Fmjgl%2Fvol19%2Fis- s1%2F1&utm_medium=PDF&utm_campaign=PDFCoverPages

15. https://www.guttmacher.org/state-policy/explore/over- view-abortion-laws

16. https://www.guttmacher.org/sites/default/files/pdfs/spibs/ spib_MWPA.pdf

GLOSSARY

abortifacient—A substance or drug that induces the body to abort a fetus.

abortion on demand / request—When a woman can simply ask for an abortion, without having to give reasons or fulfill state requirements.

cervix—The tunnel of tissue connecting the vagina to the uterus.

fertilization—Conception; when the egg cell meets the sperm cell.

fetus—A developing baby within the uterus.

gestation—The length of time and process of the fetus being carried in the uterus from conception to birth.

implantation—When the fertilized egg settles into the uterus wall.

induced abortion—Abortion; the intentional ending of a pregnancy.

infertility—The inability to produce offspring.

informed consent—Consent given voluntarily, by a competent person, able to fully understand the benefits and potential risks of their decision.

maternal mortality—Death of a woman due to pregnancy or birth-related problems.

miscarriage—The natural ending of a pregnancy before the fetus has reached full term; still-birth delivery of a baby/fetus that has died in the uterus.

obstetrics and gynecology—The branch of medicine that deals with pregnancy, childbirth, and the female reproductive system

quickening—The moment when the woman first feels the fetus move.

trimester—The first, second, or third period of three months of a pregnancy.

uterus—A hollow muscular organ located in the pelvic cavity of women and female mammals in which the fertilized egg implants and develops; also called the womb.

viability—The point at which a fetus could survive outside the woman's body.

FOR MORE INFORMATION

BOOKS

Camosy, Charles. *Beyond the Abortion Wars*. Grand Rapids, MI: Erdmans Press, 2015.

Fisher, Brian. *Abortion: The Ultimate Exploitation of Women*. New York, NY: Morgan James Publishing, 2014.

Furedi, Ann. *The Moral Case for Abortion*. New York, NY: Palgrave Macmillan, 2016

Gordon, Linda. *Woman's Body, Woman's Right*. New York, NY: Oxford UP, 1976.

Johnson, Abbey. *The Walls Are Talking: Former Abortion Clinic Workers Tell Their Stories*. San Francisco, CA: Ignatius Press, 2016

Mcbride, Doroty. *Abortion in the United States: A Reference Handbook*. New York, NY: ABC-Clio, 2008.

Pollitt, Katha. *Pro: Reclaiming Abortion Rights*. New York, NY: Picador, 2015

Schoen, Johanna. *Abortion After Roe*. Chapel Hill, NC: University of North Carolina Press, 2015

Wickilund, Susan. *This Common Secret*. New York, NY: Public Affairs, 2007.

Zeigler, Mary. *After Roe*. Cambridge, MA: Harvard University Press, 2015.

WEBSITES

National Abortion Federation (NAF)
prochoice.org
NAF is the professional association of abortion providers in North America. NAF members include private and non-profit clinics, Planned Parenthood affiliates, women's health centers, physicians' offices, and hospitals who together care for more than half the women who choose abortion in the US and Canada each year.

National Right to Life
www.nrlc.org
Founded in 1968, National Right to Life, the federation of fifty state right-to-life affiliates and more than 3,000 local chapters, is the nation's oldest and largest grassroots pro-life organization. Recognized as the flagship of the pro-life movement, NRLC works through legislation and education to protect innocent human life from abortion, infanticide, assisted suicide and euthanasia.

Planned Parenthood
www.plannedparenthood.org
In 1916, Margaret Sanger founded the Brooklyn-based American Birth Control League to provide birth control and information for women. The organization changed its name to Planned Parenthood in 1942. Today, its mission is to provide contraception, education, and health care services (including abortion), while also advocating public policy protecting these rights.

INDEX

ABOUT THE EDITOR

Anne C. Cunningham has a PhD in comparative literature and has published articles on women modernist writers and feminist theory. She currently works as an instructor of English at the University of New Mexico—Taos. She is also a songwriter and performer and lives with her husband and music partner David Lerner in Arroyo Hondo, NM.